# | Pasta |

# by Elizabeth Baird

A Madison Press Book

ISBN-10: 1-895892-92-9
ISBN-13: 978-1-895892-92-5


EDITORIAL DIRECTOR: Hugh Brewster
PROJECT EDITOR: Wanda Nowakowska
EDITORIAL ASSISTANCE: Beverley Renahan
PRODUCTION DIRECTOR: Susan Barrable
PRODUCTION COORDINATOR: Donna Chong
BOOK DESIGN AND LAYOUT: Gordon Sibley Design Inc.
COVER DESIGN: Sharon Foster
COVER PHOTOGRAPHY: Charles Schiller / FoodPix / Jupiterimages
COLOR SEPARATION: Colour Technologies
ADVISORY BOARD: Robert A. Murray, Kirk Shearer, Caren King,
Bonnie Baker Cowan, Elizabeth Baird,
Anna Hobbs


**Cook's Own: Pasta**
was produced by

MADISON PRESS BOOKS
1000 Yonge Street, Suite 200
Toronto, Ontario
Canada M4W 2K2
www.madisonpressbooks.com


*Printed in China by Lotus Printing Inc.*

# Contents

# Introduction

We're all marching to the drum of time and convenience these days. And the ingredient that's right in step with us is pasta.

Today old standbys like macaroni, spaghetti and flat noodles have been joined by radiatore, penne and farfalle, words that fall off our tongues as easily as if we were saying radiators, pens and bow ties. And fresh pasta, the dinner-party rage of a decade ago, has stayed on so deliciously that spinach fettuccine is now as available in supermarkets as bags of potatoes.

What's the cornerstone of pasta's popularity? First of all, it's so easy. Boil the pasta in a big pot of water, toss with a sauce, and presto, supper's ready. But pasta is more than just easy. It's also very satisfying, a real crowd-pleaser, and kids adore it, the simpler the better. Drizzled with tomato sauce and sprinkled with cheese, pasta is always a fail-safe supper.

Pasta can also trace its roots back to the Orient where it is found in a host of Chinese, Thai and Japanese dishes. Fast-laners call it their own when topped with five-minute mushroom sauces or tossed with a stir-fry. Sophisticated palates love to dress it up with funky goat cheese and sun-dried tomatoes or sauce it with rich Gorgonzola or smoky salmon strips and lemon.

As if this weren't enough, pasta is also inexpensive. And it plays an important role in a healthful diet.

For all of these reasons — and more — we proudly present *Cook's Own: Pasta,* bringing you everything from quick suppers to simmering sauces and splendid salads. In all, you'll find more than 100 new ways to serve delicious and pleasing pasta to family and friends.

*Elizabeth Baird*

*Capellini with Smoked Salmon and Lemon Cream Sauce (p. 32)*

TORTELLINI

SPINACH LASAGNA

LASAGNA

THIN CHINESE WHEAT NOODLES

FUSILLI LUNGHI

TUBETTI

CURLY CHINESE WHEAT NOODLES

MACARONI

ROTELLI

DITALI

FETTUCCINE

WHOLE WHEAT SPAGHETTI

CAPELLINI

SPAGHETTINI

LINGUINE

FARFALLE

RIGATONI

FETTUCCINE

STELLINI

RICE VERMICELLI

FUSILLI

RADIATORE

PENNE

RICE STICK
NOODLES

CHINESE WHEAT
NOODLES

ROTINI

BUCATINI

VERMICELLI

MEDIUM
CONCHIGLIE

JUMBO
CONCHIGLIE

MEDIUM
EGG
NOODLES

SOBA

# Presto Pastas

No wonder pasta is so popular — it cooks up quickly, tosses with almost any combination of ingredients and is ready in no time at all!

## Summer-Fresh Pasta ▶

*A quick mushroom sauté joins with fresh basil and ripe tomatoes in this simplest of all pasta sauces. Vary the sauce to suit your taste with extras such as slivered black olives, fresh parsley and chives. Or, choose fresh oyster or shiitake mushrooms for extra flavor.*

| | | |
|---|---|---|
| 1/3 cup | extra virgin olive oil | 75 mL |
| 1 | onion, chopped | 1 |
| 3 | cloves garlic, minced | 3 |
| 2 cups | sliced mushrooms (about 8 oz/250 g) | 500 mL |
| 1/4 tsp | dried thyme | 1 mL |
| 3/4 tsp | salt | 4 mL |
| 1/2 tsp | pepper | 2 mL |
| 12 oz | linguine or spaghetti | 375 g |
| 4 cups | chopped tomatoes (about 4) | 1 L |
| 1/2 cup | chopped fresh basil | 125 mL |
| | Freshly grated Parmesan cheese | |
| | Fresh basil leaves | |

● In skillet, heat 2 tbsp (25 mL) of the oil over medium heat; cook onion and garlic, stirring, for 3 minutes or until softened.

● Add mushrooms, thyme, salt and pepper; cook, stirring, for about 5 minutes or until mushrooms are softened, adding up to 1/4 cup (50 mL) water to prevent sticking.

● Meanwhile, in large pot of boiling salted water, cook linguine for 8 to 10 minutes or until tender but firm; drain well. Toss with mushroom mixture, tomatoes, remaining oil and chopped basil. Sprinkle with Parmesan to taste; garnish with basil leaves. Makes 4 servings.

**TIP:** For a delicious summer salad, cool the pasta mixture to room temperature; toss with 1 tbsp (15 mL) balsamic or red wine vinegar.

## Puttanesca with Linguine

*Once populur with streetwalkers (puttanesca), this quickly made chunky combination of tomatoes, garlic, olives and capers is now a lusty pasta classic.*

| | | |
|---|---|---|
| 2 tbsp | olive oil | 25 mL |
| 4 | cloves garlic, minced | 4 |
| 1/2 cup | each sliced Kalamata and pimiento-stuffed olives | 125 mL |
| 2 tbsp | drained capers | 25 mL |
| 1/4 tsp | each dried oregano, salt and hot pepper flakes | 1 mL |
| 1 | can (19 oz/540 mL) tomatoes | 1 |
| 1/4 cup | chopped fresh parsley | 50 mL |
| | Pepper | |
| 12 oz | linguine | 375 g |
| | Freshly grated Parmesan cheese | |

● In skillet, heat oil over medium heat; cook garlic, Kalamata and pimiento-stuffed olives, capers, oregano, salt and hot pepper flakes, stirring occasionally, for 3 minutes.

● Mash tomatoes with juice; add to skillet and bring to boil. Reduce heat and simmer for about 10 minutes or until thickened. Stir in parsley. Season with pepper to taste.

● Meanwhile, in large pot of boiling salted water, cook linguine for 8 to 10 minutes or until tender but firm; drain well. Toss with sauce; sprinkle with Parmesan to taste. Makes 4 servings.

# Oodles of Noodles

Kids just love pasta,
especially this tomato one
thickened and smoothed out
with cream cheese.

| | | |
|---|---|---|
| 1 | can (28 oz/796 mL) tomatoes | 1 |
| 1/2 cup | chopped onion | 125 mL |
| 1 tsp | dried basil (optional) | 5 mL |
| 1/4 tsp | (approx) pepper | 1 mL |
| 4 oz | light cream cheese, cubed | 125 g |
| 2-3/4 cups | macaroni or fusilli | 675 mL |
| 1/4 cup | freshly grated Parmesan cheese | 50 mL |
| | Salt | |

● In saucepan, bring tomatoes, onion, basil (if using) and pepper to boil; reduce heat and simmer for 15 minutes.

● Pour into food processor or blender; purée. Add cream cheese; purée until smooth.

● Meanwhile, in large pot of boiling salted water, cook macaroni for 8 to 10 minutes or until tender but firm; drain well. Toss with sauce; sprinkle with Parmesan. Season with salt and pepper to taste. Makes 8 servings.

# Fresh Tomato and Basil Toss

Please don't make this sauce
unless it's tomato and fresh
basil season. The charm of a
quick toss of hot pasta and
uncooked tomatoes depends
on the robust flavor of sun-
ripened tomatoes.

| | | |
|---|---|---|
| 4 cups | diced seeded tomatoes | 1 L |
| 1/2 cup | chopped fresh basil | 125 mL |
| 1/4 cup | extra virgin olive oil | 50 mL |
| 1 tsp | red wine vinegar | 5 mL |
| 3 | cloves garlic, minced | 3 |
| 1 tsp | salt | 5 mL |
| 1/2 tsp | pepper | 2 mL |
| 4 cups | rotini or penne | 1 L |
| | Freshly grated Parmesan cheese | |

● In bowl, combine tomatoes, basil, oil, vinegar, garlic, salt and pepper. *(Tomato mixture can be covered and set aside for up to 1 hour.)*

● In large pot of boiling salted water, cook rotini for 8 to 10 minutes or until tender but firm; drain well. Toss with tomato mixture; sprinkle with Parmesan to taste. Makes 4 servings.

**TIP:** Never store tomatoes in the refrigerator. The cold deadens their flavor.

# Arrabbiata

Feisty is the best way to
describe both the sauce
and its name!

| | | |
|---|---|---|
| 1 tbsp | olive oil | 15 mL |
| 1 | onion, chopped | 1 |
| 1 | zucchini, diced | 1 |
| 1 | carrot, diced | 1 |
| 1 | sweet red pepper, diced | 1 |
| 1/2 tsp | hot pepper flakes | 2 mL |
| 1/2 tsp | salt | 2 mL |
| 1/4 tsp | pepper | 1 mL |
| 1 | can (28 oz/796 mL) tomatoes, mashed | 1 |
| 12 oz | spaghetti | 375 g |
| 2 tbsp | chopped fresh parsley | 25 mL |
| | Freshly grated Parmesan cheese | |

● In large skillet, heat oil over medium heat; cook onion, zucchini, carrot, red pepper, hot pepper flakes, salt and pepper for about 5 minutes or until softened.

● Pour in tomatoes; bring to boil. Reduce heat and simmer for 10 to 15 minutes or until thickened.

● Meanwhile, in large pot of boiling salted water, cook spaghetti for 8 to 10 minutes or until tender but firm; drain well. Toss with sauce and parsley; sprinkle with Parmesan to taste. Makes 4 servings.

# Ditali in Tomato Chick-Pea Sauce

| | | |
|---|---|---|
| 2 tbsp | olive oil | 25 mL |
| 3 cups | sliced mushrooms (12 oz/375 g) | 750 mL |
| 2 | cloves garlic, minced | 2 |
| 1 | onion, finely chopped | 1 |
| 1 | can (14 oz/ 398 mL) chick-peas, drained and rinsed | 1 |
| 1 | can (28 oz/796 mL) tomatoes, chopped | 1 |
| 3/4 tsp | salt | 4 mL |
| 1/2 tsp | each pepper and dried oregano | 2 mL |
| 1-3/4 cups | ditali, penne or macaroni | 425 mL |
| 2 tbsp | chopped fresh parsley | 25 mL |
| 1/4 cup | freshly grated Parmesan cheese | 50 mL |
| | Parsley sprigs | |

● In large skillet, heat oil over medium-high heat; cook mushrooms, garlic and onion, stirring occasionally, for 10 to 15 minutes or until liquid has evaporated and mushrooms are browned.

● Stir in chick-peas, tomatoes, salt, pepper and oregano; bring to boil. Reduce heat and simmer rapidly for about 5 minutes or until slightly thickened.

● Meanwhile, in large pot of boiling salted water, cook ditali for 8 to 10 minutes or until tender but firm; drain well. Toss with sauce and parsley. Arrange on warmed serving platter; sprinkle with Parmesan. Garnish with parsley sprigs. Makes 4 servings.

*Ditali (thimbles) are short and stubby, a perfect match for a meatless sauce studded with chunky chick-peas.*

# Creamy Leek Fettuccine

| | | |
|---|---|---|
| 2 | leeks | 2 |
| 5 | slices bacon, chopped | 5 |
| 1/2 tsp | dried thyme | 2 mL |
| 1-1/2 cups | half-and-half cream | 375 mL |
| 2 oz | light cream cheese, cubed (1/4 cup/50 mL) | 50 g |
| 1 tsp | Dijon mustard | 5 mL |
| 1 tsp | pepper | 5 mL |
| 1/2 tsp | salt | 2 mL |
| 12 oz | fettuccine or linguine | 375 g |
| | Parsley sprigs | |

● Add leeks and thyme; cook, stirring occasionally, for about 5 minutes or until softened. Add cream, cream cheese, mustard, pepper and salt; bring to boil, stirring to melt cheese.

● Meanwhile, in large pot of boiling salted water, cook fettuccine for 8 to 10 minutes or until tender but firm; drain well. Toss with sauce. Arrange on warmed serving platter; garnish with reserved bacon and parsley. Makes 4 servings.

*Leeks are definitely the classy member of the onion family, but don't let the lack of leeks prevent you from trying this recipe. Just substitute two large onions and you have a delicious new variation. Cheaper, too.*

● Trim leeks and cut in half lengthwise; spread leaves and rinse thoroughly under cold water to flush out grit. Cut crosswise into thin slices.

● In skillet, cook one-quarter of the bacon over high heat until crisp; set aside for garnish. Reduce heat to medium; cook remaining bacon for 4 minutes or until limp. Drain off all but 1 tbsp (15 mL) fat.

**CLEANING LEEKS**

Since the best part of a leek is the white part, growers hill earth up around the leek as it develops in order to keep out the light and get as much white as possible. As a result, leeks harbor a lot of grit that must be removed before using.

● To clean leeks, trim off coarse outer leaves and trim down to just above the green part. Slit through the outer layers of the leek right down to the root end. Holding leeks by the root end, swish them in water, running cold water through the layers to remove dirt.

# Red Pepper Herb Pasta

*To go from a vegetable pasta dish to a vegetarian one, simply substitute vegetable stock for the chicken stock.*

| | | |
|---|---|---|
| 2 | sweet red peppers | 2 |
| 1/2 cup | chicken stock | 125 mL |
| 1/4 cup | (approx) freshly grated Parmesan cheese | 50 mL |
| 2 tbsp | cream cheese | 25 mL |
| 4 tsp | olive oil | 20 mL |
| 1/4 tsp | pepper | 1 mL |
| Pinch | hot pepper flakes (optional) | Pinch |
| 2 tbsp | each chopped fresh basil, parsley and oregano | 25 mL |
| 1 lb | fettuccine | 500 g |

● Broil red peppers, turning often, for about 20 minutes or until blistered and charred. Let cool, then peel off blackened skin; cut in half, core and seed.

● In food processor, purée red peppers, chicken stock, Parmesan, cream cheese, oil, pepper, and hot pepper flakes (if using) until smooth. Pour into saucepan; cook over medium heat for about 5 minutes or until heated through. Stir in basil, parsley and oregano.

● Meanwhile, in large pot of boiling salted water, cook fettuccine for 8 to 10 minutes or until tender but firm; drain well. Toss with sauce; sprinkle with more Parmesan to taste. Makes 4 to 6 servings.

# Tomato, Eggplant and Artichoke Spaghetti

*Eggplant adds a rich taste and texture, almost meaty in nature, to the vegetarian sauce. For the photo, we used cavatappi, a corkscrew spaghetti.*

| | | |
|---|---|---|
| 1 | eggplant (about 1 lb/500 g) | 1 |
| 1 tsp | (approx) salt | 5 mL |
| 2 tbsp | olive oil | 25 mL |
| 1/2 cup | sliced black olives | 125 mL |
| 1 | onion, chopped | 1 |
| 1 | jar (6 oz/170 mL) marinated artichokes, drained and sliced | 1 |
| 1 tbsp | capers | 15 mL |
| 2 | cloves garlic, minced | 2 |
| 1 tsp | dried oregano | 5 mL |
| 1/4 tsp | hot pepper flakes | 1 mL |
| 4 | tomatoes, peeled, seeded and chopped | 4 |
| 3 tbsp | tomato paste | 45 mL |
| 1/4 cup | chopped fresh parsley | 50 mL |
| | Pepper | |
| 1 lb | spaghetti | 500 g |
| 1/4 cup | freshly grated Parmesan cheese | 50 mL |

● Cut eggplant into 1/2-inch (1 cm) cubes. In colander, sprinkle eggplant with salt. Let stand for 30 minutes. Rinse and pat dry.

● In large heavy saucepan, heat oil over medium heat; cook olives, onion, artichokes, capers, garlic, oregano and hot pepper flakes, stirring, for 4 minutes or until onion is softened.

● Stir in eggplant, tomatoes and tomato paste; cover and cook, stirring often, for about 15 minutes or until eggplant is tender and sauce has thickened. Stir in parsley, and salt and pepper to taste.

● Meanwhile, in large pot of boiling salted water, cook spaghetti for 8 to 10 minutes or until tender but firm; drain well. Toss with sauce; sprinkle with Parmesan. Makes 4 to 6 servings.

*(clockwise from top) Zucchini Carrot Pasta (p. 14); Tomato, Eggplant and Artichoke Spaghetti; Red Pepper Herb Pasta.*

# Zucchini Carrot Pasta

*Two stars from the summer garden team up with pretty bow-tie pasta for a dish that's ready in minutes (photo, p. 13).*

| | | |
|---|---|---|
| 2 tbsp | olive oil | 25 mL |
| 1 cup | chopped red onion | 250 mL |
| 3 | cloves garlic, minced | 3 |
| 3 cups | each sliced carrots and zucchini | 750 mL |
| 1 cup | vegetable stock | 250 mL |
| 8 cups | farfalle | 2 L |
| 1 cup | freshly grated Parmesan cheese | 250 mL |
| 1/2 tsp | pepper | 2 mL |
| | Salt | |
| 1/4 cup | each chopped fresh parsley and basil | 50 mL |

● In skillet, heat oil over medium-high heat; cook onion and garlic, stirring, for about 3 minutes or until softened.

● Add carrots; cook, stirring, for 2 minutes. Add zucchini; cook, stirring, for 3 minutes. Pour in stock and bring to boil; cook for 2 minutes.

● Meanwhile, in large pot of boiling salted water, cook farfalle for 8 to 10 minutes or until tender but firm; drain and return to pot. Stir in vegetable mixture, Parmesan, pepper, and salt to taste. Gently toss with parsley and basil. Makes 6 servings.

# Olive and Sun-Dried Tomato Spaghettini

*The success of this simple pasta toss depends on the best olive oil (see sidebar, p. 19) and black olives. Avoid canned black olives; they're too bland. Instead, choose black olives with oomph — available in bulk in Italian, Greek and Portuguese grocery stores as well as in some specialty shops and supermarkets.*

| | | |
|---|---|---|
| 1 lb | spaghettini | 500 g |
| 1/2 cup | extra virgin olive oil | 125 mL |
| 4 | cloves garlic, minced | 4 |
| 1/4 tsp | hot pepper flakes | 1 mL |
| 1/2 cup | black olives, cut into large pieces | 125 mL |
| 1/4 cup | drained oil-packed sun-dried tomatoes, cut into strips | 50 mL |
| 1 tsp | salt | 5 mL |
| 1/4 tsp | pepper | 1 mL |
| 1/4 cup | chopped fresh basil or parsley | 50 mL |

● In large pot of boiling salted water, cook spaghettini for 8 to 10 minutes or until tender but firm; drain well.

● Meanwhile, in large skillet, heat half of the oil over medium heat; cook garlic and hot pepper flakes for 2 to 3 minutes or until fragrant but not browned.

● Add olives, tomatoes, salt and pepper; cook for 2 to 3 minutes or until heated through. Add to pasta along with remaining oil and basil; toss well. Makes 6 servings.

**TIP:** If sun-dried tomatoes are unavailable, substitute 3/4 cup (175 mL) chopped fresh tomatoes and cook them with the garlic and hot pepper flakes for 3 to 4 minutes before adding the olives.

## OLIVES

● Olives are picked either unripe (green), almost ripe (red to black), or ripe (black). They are virtually inedible until they are cured. Commercial methods of curing olives include soaking them in olive oil, water, brine or salt for several months; dry-curing them in salt; or lye-curing them in a strong alkaline solution and then rinsing thoroughly, which is the most common method used.

● Whenever possible, taste olives before you buy them. In grocery stores specializing in foods from Greece, Italy and the Middle East, olives are often sold in bulk in bins. Most shopkeepers offer samples to buying customers.

● Choose from tangy pointy purple Kalamata olives, mellower dry-cured black olives which are excellent for cooking, tiny Niçoise olives packed in olive oil and jumbo greens so beloved for snacking.

● Supermarkets provide choices, too, especially in jarred olives, but avoid canned ripe olives — they get the prize for bland!

# Kasha and Bows ▲

| 1/3 cup | butter | 75 mL |
|---|---|---|
| 2 | onions, chopped | 2 |
| 1 cup | kasha | 250 mL |
| 1 | egg, beaten | 1 |
| 2 cups | boiling water | 500 mL |
| 1 tsp | salt | 5 mL |
| 1/4 tsp | pepper | 1 mL |
| 4 cups | farfalle or macaroni | 1 L |

● In skillet, melt butter over medium heat; cook onions for 10 to 15 minutes or until browned and crisp.

● Meanwhile, in saucepan, cook kasha with egg over medium heat, stirring, for about 2 minutes or until kasha seems dry. Add water, salt and pepper; reduce heat, cover and simmer for about 10 minutes or until kasha is tender and liquid is absorbed.

● Meanwhile, in large pot of boiling salted water, cook farfalle for 8 to 10 minutes or until tender but firm; drain well and toss with kasha and onions. Makes 6 servings.

**TIP:** Adding an egg to the kasha before it is cooked separates the grains and gives a nice texture.

K*asha (hulled kernels of buckwheat) tossed with farfalle doubles as a satisfying main dish or side dish. For our photograph, we used red onions and cooked them until tender but not browned.*

# Penne with Swiss Chard, Raisins and Pine Nuts ▲

*B*oth *Swiss chard and rapini, if you prefer it, have a pleasant bitterness that's perfectly in balance with the sweetness of raisins and the meatiness of pine nuts.*

| 1 lb | Swiss chard (or rapini) | 500 g |
|------|-------------------------|-------|
| 1/3 cup | extra virgin olive oil | 75 mL |
| 1 | onion, chopped | 1 |
| 3 | cloves garlic, minced | 3 |
| 3/4 tsp | salt | 4 mL |
| 1/2 tsp | pepper | 2 mL |
| Pinch | hot pepper flakes | Pinch |
| 1/2 cup | raisins | 125 mL |
| 1 tbsp | balsamic or red wine vinegar | 15 mL |
| 4 cups | penne | 1 L |
| 1/3 cup | toasted pine nuts | 75 mL |

● Separate Swiss chard into ribs and leaves; cut into 1-inch (2.5 cm) pieces. In large pot of boiling salted water, cook Swiss chard ribs for 7 minutes. Add leaves and cook for 3 minutes. Drain and refresh under cold water. Drain and set aside.

● In large skillet, heat oil over medium heat; cook onion, garlic, salt, pepper and hot pepper flakes for 5 minutes or until softened. Add Swiss chard, raisins and vinegar; toss together.

● Meanwhile, in large pot of boiling salted water, cook penne for 8 to 10 minutes or until tender but firm. Drain and toss with Swiss chard mixture. Garnish with pine nuts. Makes 4 servings.

# Tomato and Eggplant Whole Wheat Spaghetti

| | | |
|---|---|---|
| 1 | eggplant (about 1 lb/500 g) | 1 |
| 1 tsp | salt | 5 mL |
| 4 tsp | vegetable oil | 20 mL |
| 1 | large onion, chopped | 1 |
| 2 | cloves garlic, minced | 2 |
| 2 tbsp | water | 25 mL |
| 1 | can (28 oz/796 mL) tomatoes, crushed | 1 |
| 2 tsp | dried basil | 10 mL |
| Pinch | hot pepper flakes | Pinch |
| | Salt and pepper | |
| 12 oz | whole wheat spaghetti | 375 g |
| 2 tbsp | chopped fresh parsley | 25 mL |
| 2 tbsp | freshly grated Parmesan cheese | 25 mL |

● Cut eggplant into 1/2-inch (1 cm) cubes. In colander, sprinkle eggplant with salt. Let stand for 30 minutes. Rinse and pat dry.

● In saucepan, heat oil over medium-high heat; cook eggplant, stirring, for 2 minutes. Add onion, garlic and water; cook for 3 minutes.

● Add tomatoes, basil and hot pepper flakes; bring to boil. Reduce heat and simmer for 20 to 30 minutes or until thickened and eggplant is tender. Season with salt and pepper to taste.

● Meanwhile, in large pot of boiling salted water, cook spaghetti for 8 to 10 minutes or until tender but firm; drain well. Toss with sauce, parsley and Parmesan. Makes 4 servings.

*Eggplant may seem like an ordinary vegetable until you taste what it does to a simple tomato sauce — adding a satisfying meatiness that the basil and hot pepper flakes accent.*

# Creamy Rotini with Asparagus

| | | |
|---|---|---|
| 1 lb | fresh asparagus | 500 g |
| 1/4 cup | butter, melted | 50 mL |
| 1 | clove garlic, minced | 1 |
| 2 | shallots, finely chopped | 2 |
| 1 cup | whipping cream | 250 mL |
| 3/4 cup | creamy goat cheese (chèvre), cubed | 175 mL |
| 1 tsp | grated lemon rind | 5 mL |
| 2 tbsp | lemon juice | 25 mL |
| | Salt and pepper | |
| 4 cups | rotini or penne | 1 L |
| 1/4 cup | freshly grated Parmesan cheese | 50 mL |
| 1/4 cup | slivered black olives | 50 mL |
| 3 | green onions, sliced | 3 |

● Snap tough ends off asparagus and discard; cut stalks diagonally into 1-inch (2.5 cm) pieces. In saucepan, bring 1/2 cup (125 mL) water to boil; add asparagus and cook for 2 to 3 minutes or until tender-crisp. Drain well and set aside.

● In saucepan, heat 2 tbsp (25 mL) of the butter over medium heat; cook garlic and shallots for about 2 minutes or until softened. Add cream and bring to boil; reduce heat to simmer.

● Whisk in goat cheese, lemon rind and juice until smooth. Season with salt and pepper to taste. Stir in asparagus; cook until heated through.

● Meanwhile, in large pot of boiling salted water, cook rotini for 8 to 10 minutes or until tender but firm; drain well. Toss with remaining butter; toss with sauce. Transfer to warmed serving platter; sprinkle with Parmesan, olives and green onions. Makes 8 appetizer servings.

*Asparagus stars in an easy springtime appetizer. You can omit the olives and use one small onion instead of the shallots.*

# New-Style Pasta Primavera

*In this new version of a pasta classic, the whipping cream has been abandoned in favor of lots of herbs, lemon juice and quick cooking which retains flavors and textures.*

| | | |
|---|---|---|
| 2 tbsp | butter | 25 mL |
| 2 | cloves garlic, minced | 2 |
| 2 | zucchini, chopped | 2 |
| 2 | carrots, chopped | 2 |
| 1 | sweet red pepper, chopped | 1 |
| 1 | onion, cut into thin wedges | 1 |
| 1 lb | asparagus or broccoli, cut into 1-1/2-inch (4 cm) pieces | 500 g |
| 1-1/2 cups | peas | 375 mL |
| 1 cup | canned chicken broth (undiluted) | 250 mL |
| 3 tbsp | each chopped fresh chives and oregano | 50 mL |
| 1 tsp | salt | 5 mL |
| 3/4 tsp | pepper | 4 mL |
| 12 oz | fusilli lunghi | 375 g |
| 1/2 cup | freshly grated Parmesan cheese | 125 mL |
| 2 tbsp | chopped fresh parsley | 25 mL |
| 1 tbsp | lemon juice | 15 mL |

● In large skillet, melt butter over medium heat; cook garlic, zucchini, carrots, red pepper, onion and asparagus, stirring occasionally, for 3 minutes.

● Add peas, chicken stock, chives and oregano; bring to boil. Reduce heat and simmer for 5 minutes or until vegetables are tender-crisp. Stir in salt and pepper.

● Meanwhile, in large pot of boiling salted water, cook fusilli for 8 to 10 minutes or until tender but firm; drain well. Toss with vegetable mixture. Sprinkle with Parmesan and parsley; toss again. Sprinkle with lemon juice; toss again. Makes 4 to 6 servings.

# Aglio e Olio

*Garlic and olive oil create all the sauce you need for this traditional old-country pasta. This is one recipe where the quality of the olive oil really counts (see sidebar, next page).*

| | | |
|---|---|---|
| 1/2 cup | extra virgin olive oil | 125 mL |
| 8 | cloves garlic, minced | 8 |
| 1 tsp | salt | 5 mL |
| 1/2 tsp | hot pepper flakes | 2 mL |
| 12 oz | spaghetti | 375 g |
| 1/3 cup | chopped fresh parsley | 75 mL |
| | Pepper | |

● In small saucepan or skillet, heat oil over low heat; cook garlic, salt and hot pepper flakes, watching carefully and stirring occasionally, for about 15 minutes or until garlic is light golden but not browned.

● Meanwhile, in large pot of boiling salted water, cook spaghetti for 8 to 10 minutes or until tender but firm; drain well.

● Toss with oil mixture and parsley. Season with pepper to taste. Makes 4 servings.

VARIATION

TOASTED CRUMBS AND GARLIC: Reduce hot pepper flakes to 1/4 tsp (1 mL). Coarsely crumble enough crustless Italian or French bread to make 2 cups (500 mL) fresh crumbs. Toast in 350°F (180°C) oven for 8 minutes or until crisp and golden. Prepare Aglio e Olio as above, adding crumbs to pasta along with oil mixture.

# Presto Pesto

| | | |
|---|---|---|
| 2 cups | packed fresh basil leaves | 500 mL |
| 1/2 cup | freshly grated Parmesan cheese | 125 mL |
| 1/4 cup | pine nuts | 50 mL |
| 3/4 cup | extra virgin olive oil | 175 mL |
| 3 | cloves garlic, minced | 3 |

● In food processor, finely chop basil, Parmesan and pine nuts.

● With motor running, gradually add oil in thin steady stream. Stir in garlic. Makes 1 cup (250 mL).

**TIP:** It's always a good idea to save a little of the pasta cooking water to thin out the pesto as you are tossing it with the pasta.

*August is the time to whirl up batches of pesto and freeze them in containers just the right size for a bowl of pasta. This recipe makes enough to toss with about 1-1/2 lb (750 g) long pasta and serve six.*

## OLIVE OILS

*Buying olive oil can be confusing — so many types from so many countries and for such a price range. Here are a some suggestions that will help you make the right choice.*

● All olive oil is made from olives, the fruit of the olive tree, and most come from countries around the Mediterranean where olives have been cultivated for about 6,000 years.

● Oil released from the first grinding and pressing of olives is superior — fruitier, more robust and low in acid. Look for **extra virgin** on the label for this oil but note that, even among the extra virgin bottles, which must have less than 1% acidity, differences in quality exist. Some producers blend oils to lower the acid level of their lesser-quality oil, enabling these bottles to be labeled "extra virgin" as well.

● The best advice is to look for the words "**cold pressed**" or "**first cold pressing**" when looking for **quality extra virgin olive oil**. Understandably, this cold-pressed oil is more expensive, but it is an oil you use sparingly, reserving it for pasta dishes such as Aglio e Olio (p. 18) or Presto Pesto (this page) where the taste and presence of the olive oil really matter. Use it, too, for dressing salads and cooked vegetables, dipping crusty sourdough bread or as a table condiment.

● Lower in price is **pure olive oil**, made from the second or third pressing of the olives. This rather bland oil has been treated to lower its acid level, and lacks the characteristic olive flavor and color. However, it can be used in frying or in any dish where you want a neutral oil.

● So-called "**light**" **olive oil** is not lighter in calories, simply lighter in color and flavor.

● Store unopened olive oil in a dark, cool place for up to 2 years. Once opened, use up the bottle within 2 months, storing it as before.

# Mushroom Tofu Noodles ▲

A *warm golden egg noodle, available fresh in Oriental grocery stores, tastes terrific with this vegetarian topping, but other pasta types such as fusilli taste just fine, too. Toasting the almonds adds so much oomph to the dish that you shouldn't miss that step.*

| | | |
|---|---|---|
| 1 tbsp | vegetable oil | 15 mL |
| 2 | cloves garlic, minced | 2 |
| 1 | large onion, chopped | 1 |
| 3 cups | thinly sliced mushrooms (12 oz/375 g) | 750 mL |
| Half | each sweet red and green pepper, diced | Half |
| 1/2 cup | vegetable stock | 125 mL |
| 1/4 cup | tamari or soy sauce | 50 mL |
| 1 tsp | ginger | 5 mL |
| 2 tsp | cornstarch | 10 mL |
| 1 lb | firm tofu, grated | 500 g |
| 1 | pkg (12 oz/350 g) steamed Chinese noodles | 1 |
| 1/2 cup | slivered almonds, toasted (see TIP, p. 25) | 125 mL |
| 4 | green onions, chopped | 4 |

● In skillet, heat oil over medium heat; cook garlic and onion for about 3 minutes or until softened.

● Stir in mushrooms, red and green peppers, stock, tamari and ginger until coated. Reduce heat and simmer, covered, for about 5 minutes or until mushrooms are softened.

● Blend cornstarch with 1 tbsp (15 mL) water; stir into skillet. Mix in tofu; cover and simmer for about 5 minutes or until heated through.

● Meanwhile, in large pot of boiling salted water, cook noodles for about 2 minutes or until tender but firm; drain well. Arrange on warmed serving platter. Top with tofu mixture; sprinkle with almonds and green onions. Makes 4 servings.

# Linguine with Wild Mushroom Sauce

| | | |
|---|---|---|
| 1/2 oz | dried porcini mushrooms | 15 g |
| 1 tbsp | butter | 15 mL |
| 1 | onion, chopped | 1 |
| 3 | cloves garlic, minced | 3 |
| 1/2 tsp | dried thyme | 2 mL |
| 1/2 tsp | salt | 2 mL |
| 1/4 tsp | pepper | 1 mL |
| 1 cup | sliced fresh mushrooms (4 oz/125 g) | 250 mL |
| 1 cup | whipping cream | 250 mL |
| 1/4 cup | freshly grated Parmesan cheese | 50 mL |
| 12 oz | linguine | 375 g |

● Rinse dried mushrooms under cold water. Soak for 15 minutes in 1/2 cup (125 mL) boiling water. Strain through cheesecloth-lined sieve, reserving liquid. Rinse mushrooms; chop coarsely.

● In skillet, melt butter over medium heat; cook onion, garlic, porcini mushrooms, thyme, salt and pepper for 3 minutes or until softened.

● Add fresh mushrooms and reserved soaking liquid; cook for 2 minutes. Pour in cream and bring to boil; boil for 2 minutes or until slightly thickened. Remove from heat; stir in Parmesan.

● Meanwhile, in large pot of boiling salted water, cook linguine for 8 to 10 minutes or until tender but firm; drain well. Toss with sauce. Makes 4 servings.

*Porcini mushrooms, available dried in delis and Italian grocery stores, deliver such a wonderful cascade of taste with each bite that they're worth every penny for this special-occasion pasta.*

# Saucy Parmesan Pasta with Asparagus

| | | |
|---|---|---|
| 1 lb | fresh asparagus | 500 g |
| 2 tbsp | butter | 25 mL |
| 1/3 cup | chopped green onions | 75 mL |
| 2 tbsp | all-purpose flour | 25 mL |
| 1/4 tsp | each pepper and nutmeg | 1 mL |
| 1-3/4 cups | milk | 425 mL |
| 3/4 cup | freshly grated Parmesan cheese | 175 mL |
| 12 oz | fusilli or penne | 375 g |

● Snap tough ends off asparagus and discard; cut stalks diagonally into 1-inch (2.5 cm) pieces. In saucepan, bring 1/2 cup (125 mL) water to boil; add asparagus and cook for 2 to 3 minutes or until tender-crisp. Drain well and set aside.

● In same saucepan, melt butter over medium heat; cook onions, stirring, for 3 minutes or until softened. Stir in flour, pepper and nutmeg; cook for 1 minute. Gradually whisk in milk until smooth; cook, whisking, for 3 to 5 minutes or until boiling and thickened. Stir in Parmesan until melted.

● Meanwhile, in large pot of boiling salted water, cook fusilli for 8 to 10 minutes or until tender but firm; drain well. Toss with sauce and asparagus. Makes 4 servings.

VARIATION
SAUCY CHEDDAR PASTA: Substitute Cheddar cheese for the Parmesan. Season with salt and pepper to taste.

*The base of this pleasing dish is a cream sauce accented with nutmeg.*

# Gourmand's Gorgonzola Linguine

*Indulgent, special-occasion, worth every last calorie! — they all apply to this creamy, cheesy sauce.*

| | | |
|---|---|---|
| 12 oz | linguine or spaghetti | 375 g |
| 1 cup | whipping cream | 250 mL |
| 1 tbsp | butter | 15 mL |
| 6 oz | Gorgonzola cheese, crumbled | 175 g |
| 1/4 cup | (approx) freshly grated Parmesan cheese | 50 mL |
| 1/2 tsp | (approx) pepper | 2 mL |
| | Salt | |

● In large pot of boiling salted water, cook linguine for 8 to 10 minutes or until tender but firm; drain well.

● Meanwhile, in heavy saucepan, bring cream and butter to boil; boil for 1 minute. Reduce heat to low; stir in Gorgonzola until melted. Stir in Parmesan and pepper; toss with pasta.

● Arrange on warmed serving platter; sprinkle with more Parmesan, salt and pepper to taste. Makes 4 servings.

# Fettuccine Alfredo — The Classic

*For some reason, this is a favorite party dish for kids. It must be the meltingly mild and smooth sauce with a hint of nutmeg — the same reason adults can't wait to dig into a bowl of classic Alfredo!*

| | | |
|---|---|---|
| 12 oz | fettuccine | 375 g |
| 1 cup | whipping cream | 250 mL |
| 1/4 cup | butter | 50 mL |
| 1 cup | freshly grated Parmesan cheese | 250 mL |
| 1/2 tsp | salt | 2 mL |
| 1/4 tsp | pepper | 1 mL |
| Pinch | nutmeg | Pinch |
| | Parsley sprigs | |

● In large pot of boiling salted water, cook fettuccine for 8 to 10 minutes or until tender but firm; drain well.

● Meanwhile, in large saucepan or skillet, bring cream and butter just to boil. Reduce heat and stir in Parmesan, salt, pepper and nutmeg; toss with pasta. Arrange on warmed serving platter; garnish with parsley. Makes 4 servings.

## THE BEST CHEESES FOR PASTA

*Cheeses with character and/or creaminess are the best matches for pasta. Old Cheddar, Gruyère, Emmenthal, Gorgonzola, feta and creamy goat cheese (chèvre) all add enough distinctly robust taste to carry off pasta's background blandness. Here's more on some of the most popular cheeses for pasta.*

● **Parmesan**: Parmigiano Reggiano is the authentic grainy cheese from the area around Parma, Italy. Although it is more expensive than its imitators, a little of its magnificent full taste goes a long way. A wedge of it keeps in the refrigerator for weeks, at the ready to grate over pasta. Avoid pre-grated Parmesan as it is usually dry and often acrid.

● **Mozzarella**: This ivory-colored unripened cheese gives creaminess and stretch, especially to baked pastas where other stronger ingredients make up for its mildness.

● **Provolone**: A stretchy cheese that starts out mild with a bit of an edge but becomes strong, tangy and robust as it ages, provolone blends well with other cheeses and gives depth to their flavor.

● **Ricotta**: This soft and moist, slightly granular unripened cheese has a milky taste and comes in varying degrees of milk fat. It is often used in stuffed or baked pasta, and is sold in tubs, like yogurt or sour cream.

● **Asiago**: This sharp hard cheese is wonderful shaved over pasta. Use as you would Parmigiano Reggiano.

● **Pecorino Romano**: Grate this pungent cheese over pasta and to make a crusty top on baked pasta dishes. Use as you would Parmigiano Reggiano.

# Alfredo's Leaner Fettuccine

| | | |
|---|---|---|
| 12 oz | fettuccine or linguine | 375 g |
| 1 cup | 2% cottage cheese | 250 mL |
| 1/3 cup | freshly grated Parmesan cheese | 75 mL |
| 1/4 cup | 2% milk | 50 mL |
| 1/4 tsp | each salt and pepper | 1 mL |
| Pinch | nutmeg | Pinch |
| | Parsley sprigs | |

● In large pot of boiling salted water, cook fettuccine for 8 to 10 minutes or until tender but firm; drain well and return to pot.

● Meanwhile, in food processor, purée cottage cheese until smooth. Add Parmesan, milk, salt, pepper and nutmeg; blend until smooth.

● Add to drained pasta; cook over medium heat, stirring constantly, for 1 minute. Arrange on warmed serving platter; garnish with parsley. Makes 4 servings.

*While special occasions let us indulge, everyday eating should be as lean as possible. Here's how our Test Kitchen trimmed off fat and calories from the classic Alfredo, and still came up with a wonderfully satisfying and great-tasting dish.*

# Instant Mac and Cheese

| | | |
|---|---|---|
| 1-1/2 cups | macaroni | 375 mL |
| 1 cup | shredded Cheddar cheese | 250 mL |
| 1/4 cup | plain yogurt | 50 mL |
| 1 tbsp | butter | 15 mL |
| 1 tbsp | Dijon mustard | 15 mL |
| 1/4 tsp | each salt and pepper | 1 mL |
| Pinch | hot pepper flakes | Pinch |

● In large pot of boiling salted water, cook macaroni for about 8 to 10 minutes or until tender but firm; drain well.

● Meanwhile, in bowl, stir together Cheddar and yogurt; set aside.

● In same pot over low heat, melt butter; stir in mustard, salt, pepper and hot pepper flakes. Add macaroni and toss to coat. Remove from heat; add cheese mixture and toss. Makes 2 servings.

*You know those boxed macaroni and cheese suppers that are ready so fast and are so good for filling tummies? Well, this one takes only seconds longer to prepare — and tastes much, much better. You'll never go back to boxed again!*

# Macaroni with Four Cheeses

| | | |
|---|---|---|
| 3/4 cup | shredded mozzarella cheese | 175 mL |
| 3/4 cup | shredded Cheddar cheese | 175 mL |
| 3/4 cup | shredded Gruyère cheese | 175 mL |
| 1/3 cup | freshly grated Parmesan cheese | 75 mL |
| 2-3/4 cups | macaroni | 675 mL |
| 3/4 cup | light cream | 175 mL |
| | Chopped fresh parsley | |
| | Pepper | |

● In bowl, combine mozzarella, Cheddar, Gruyère and half of the Parmesan; set aside.

● In large pot of boiling salted water, cook macaroni for 8 to 10 minutes or until tender but firm; drain well and return to pot.

● Add cheese mixture and cream; cook over low heat for 1 minute or until cheese has melted. Sprinkle with remaining Parmesan, and parsley to taste. Season with pepper to taste. Makes 4 servings.

*Mozzarella gives you lusciously gooey stretch, Cheddar and Parmesan touch the flavor high notes and Swiss Gruyère fills in the mellow background.*

# Garden-Fresh Spaghetti ▼

*Chopped sweet pepper and tomatoes, added at the end of the cooking time, give the beef sauce freshness and crunch.*

| | | |
|---|---|---|
| 1 tbsp | vegetable oil | 15 mL |
| 1 lb | ground beef | 500 g |
| 1 | onion, chopped | 1 |
| Half | stalk celery, diced | Half |
| 3 | cloves garlic, minced | 3 |
| 1 | can (28 oz/796 mL) tomato sauce | 1 |
| 1-1/2 tsp | each dried basil and oregano | 7 mL |
| 1/2 tsp | salt | 2 mL |
| Pinch | pepper | Pinch |
| 2 | tomatoes, chopped | 2 |

| | | |
|---|---|---|
| 1 | sweet yellow, red or green pepper, diced | 1 |
| 1 lb | spaghetti | 500 g |
| 1 cup | shredded mozzarella cheese | 250 mL |
| 1/4 cup | freshly grated Parmesan cheese | 50 mL |

● In large deep skillet, heat oil over medium heat; cook beef, onion, celery and garlic, stirring, for 5 minutes or until meat is browned. Drain off fat.

● Add tomato sauce, basil, oregano, salt and pepper; bring to boil. Reduce heat, cover and simmer for 15 minutes. Stir in tomatoes and sweet pepper.

● Meanwhile, in large pot of boiling salted water, cook spaghetti for 8 to 10 minutes or until tender but firm; drain well. Toss with sauce. Sprinkle with mozzarella and Parmesan. Makes 4 to 6 servings.

# Very Tomato and Chicken Ragu

| | | |
|---|---|---|
| 1 tbsp | olive oil | 15 mL |
| 1 | onion, chopped | 1 |
| 2 | cloves garlic, minced | 2 |
| 1-1/2 tsp | dried basil | 7 mL |
| 1/2 tsp | dried oregano | 2 mL |
| 1/4 tsp | hot pepper flakes | 1 mL |
| 1 lb | ground chicken | 500 g |
| 1 | can (28 oz/796 mL) tomatoes | 1 |
| 1/4 cup | tomato paste | 50 mL |
| 2 tbsp | chopped sun-dried tomatoes | 25 mL |
| 1 tsp | salt | 5 mL |
| 1/4 tsp | pepper | 1 mL |
| 12 oz | spaghetti or spaghettini | 375 g |
| | Freshly grated Parmesan cheese | |

● In large skillet, heat oil over medium heat; cook onion, garlic, basil, oregano and hot pepper flakes, stirring, for 3 minutes or until softened.

● Add ground chicken; cook, breaking up into large chunks, for 5 to 8 minutes or until no longer pink. Drain off any fat.

● Add tomatoes, breaking up into chunks, tomato paste, sun-dried tomatoes, salt and pepper; bring to boil. Reduce heat and simmer for 20 minutes or until thickened.

● Meanwhile, in large pot of boiling salted water, cook spaghetti for 8 to 10 minutes or until tender but firm; drain well. Toss with sauce. Sprinkle with Parmesan to taste. Makes 4 servings.

*Very tomato, because the sauce contains tomatoes three ways — canned, paste and sun-dried.*

# Chicken Curry Pasta

| | | |
|---|---|---|
| 2 tbsp | vegetable oil | 25 mL |
| 2 | cloves garlic, minced | 2 |
| 1 | onion, chopped | 1 |
| 1 tbsp | curry powder | 15 mL |
| 1/4 tsp | each paprika and ginger | 1 mL |
| 1 lb | boneless skinless chicken breasts, slivered | 500 g |
| 1-1/4 cups | chicken stock | 300 mL |
| 2 tbsp | tomato paste | 25 mL |
| 1/3 cup | raisins | 75 mL |
| 1/3 cup | plain yogurt | 75 mL |
| 1/2 tsp | salt | 2 mL |
| 1/4 tsp | pepper | 1 mL |
| 4 cups | penne | 1 L |
| 1/4 cup | chopped fresh coriander or parsley | 50 mL |
| 1/4 cup | chopped peanuts or almonds, toasted (see TIP below) | 50 mL |

● In large skillet, heat oil over medium-high heat; cook garlic and onion for 2 minutes or until softened. Add curry powder, paprika and ginger; cook, stirring, for 1 minute. Add chicken; cook, stirring, for 3 minutes or until lightly browned.

● Stir in 1/4 cup (50 mL) of the stock; cook for 1 minute or until evaporated. Add remaining stock and tomato paste; bring to boil. Reduce heat and sprinkle with raisins; simmer for 5 minutes or until chicken is no longer pink inside. Remove from heat; stir in yogurt, salt and pepper.

● Meanwhile, in large pot of boiling salted water, cook penne for 8 to 10 minutes or until tender but firm; drain well. Toss with sauce; arrange on warmed serving platter. Garnish with coriander and peanuts. Makes 4 servings.

*Italy meets India in a deliciously different pasta dish with a spicy-sweet taste. Top each serving with a dollop of yogurt.*

**TIP:** To toast peanuts or almonds, cook in small skillet over medium-low heat for 3 to 5 minutes or until golden.

# Cheesy Chicken Fettuccine

*Kids will love this mild
pasta sauce. For sophisticated
palates, replace most of
the mozzarella with gutsier
provolone.*

| 2 tbsp | olive oil | 25 mL |
|---|---|---|
| 1 lb | boneless skinless chicken breasts, slivered | 500 g |
| 1/2 tsp | dried rosemary | 2 mL |
| 1/4 cup | chicken stock | 50 mL |
| 1 tbsp | all-purpose flour | 15 mL |
| 1-1/2 cups | milk | 375 mL |
| 1-1/2 cups | frozen peas | 375 mL |
| 1/2 cup | each shredded mozzarella and provolone cheeses | 125 mL |
| 1/4 cup | freshly grated Parmesan cheese | 50 mL |
| 1/4 cup | chopped fresh parsley | 50 mL |
| 1/4 tsp | each salt and pepper | 1 mL |
| 12 oz | fettuccine | 375 g |

● In large skillet, heat oil over medium-high heat; cook chicken and rosemary, stirring, for about 5 minutes or until golden brown. Remove from skillet and set aside.

● Pour stock into skillet, stirring to scrape up any brown bits; cook for about 1 minute or until reduced to 1 tbsp (15 mL).

● Sprinkle with flour; stir until smooth. Stir in milk and peas; bring to boil, stirring.

● Remove from heat; gradually whisk in mozzarella, provolone and Parmesan until smooth. Stir in chicken, parsley, salt and pepper.

● Meanwhile, in large pot of boiling salted water, cook fettuccine for 8 to 10 minutes or until tender but firm; drain well. Toss with sauce. Makes 4 servings.

# Oriental Stir-Fry Pasta

*Stir-fries over rice are old
hat. Over pasta, they're new
to us, but quite authentic. If
you can find fresh Chinese
noodles (available in various
widths and colors), sold
vacuum-packed in Oriental
shops, do use them in this
recipe. Since they're fresh,
you'll need about 1 lb (500 g).*

| 1 | each carrot and stalk celery | 1 |
|---|---|---|
| 3 | boneless skinless chicken breasts | 3 |
| 1 tbsp | olive oil | 15 mL |
| 1 | small onion, chopped | 1 |
| 2 tbsp | minced gingerroot | 25 mL |
| 2 | cloves garlic, minced | 2 |
| 1 cup | sliced mushrooms (4 oz/125 g) | 250 mL |
| 2 cups | trimmed snow peas | 500 mL |
| 1 | sweet red pepper, cut into thin strips | 1 |
| 2 tbsp | dry sherry | 25 mL |
| 1/4 cup | oyster sauce | 50 mL |
| 2 tbsp | soy sauce | 25 mL |
| 1 tsp | sesame oil | 5 mL |
| Pinch | hot pepper flakes | Pinch |
| 8 oz | spaghettini | 250 g |
| 1 tbsp | sesame seeds | 15 mL |

● Thinly slice carrot and celery on diagonal; set aside. Cut chicken into strips.

● In wok or large skillet, heat oil over medium-high heat; cook chicken, stirring, for 3 minutes or until browned. Transfer to plate and set aside.

● Add carrot, celery, onion, ginger and garlic to wok; cook, stirring, for 3 minutes or until softened. Add mushrooms; cook for 1 minute.

● Return chicken to wok along with snow peas, red pepper and sherry; cover and cook for 4 minutes or until chicken is no longer pink inside. Stir in oyster sauce, soy sauce, sesame oil and hot pepper flakes, mixing well.

● Meanwhile, in large pot of boiling salted water, cook spaghettini for 8 to 10 minutes or until tender but firm; drain well. Toss with chicken mixture; sprinkle with sesame seeds. Makes 4 servings.

# Penne with Creamy Tomato Sauce

| 4 | slices bacon, diced (about 4 oz/125 g) | 4 |
| 1 | onion, chopped | 1 |
| 1 | can (19 oz/540 mL) tomatoes | 1 |
| 1/2 cup | whipping cream | 125 mL |
| 1/4 cup | vodka (optional) | 50 mL |
| 4 cups | penne | 1 L |
| | Salt and pepper | |
| 1/2 cup | freshly grated Parmesan cheese | 125 mL |

● In large saucepan, cook bacon over medium heat for 3 minutes. Add onion; cook for 2 to 3 minutes or until softened.

● Add tomatoes and mash with potato masher; bring to boil. Reduce heat and simmer for 20 minutes or until thickened slightly. Stir in cream; simmer for 5 minutes longer. Stir in vodka (if using).

● Meanwhile, in large pot of boiling salted water, cook penne for 8 to 10 minutes or until tender but firm; drain well. Toss with sauce; season with salt and pepper to taste. Sprinkle with Parmesan. Makes 4 servings.

*Bacon adds a wonderful smoky flavor to this special-occasion dish.*

# Amatriciana

| 8 oz | pancetta or bacon (in one piece), diced | 250 g |
| 1 | onion, chopped | 1 |
| 1/2 tsp | hot pepper flakes | 2 mL |
| 1/4 tsp | each salt and pepper | 1 mL |
| 1 | can (28 oz/796 mL) tomatoes, puréed | 1 |
| 1/2 cup | freshly grated Parmesan cheese | 125 mL |
| 12 oz | bucatini or spaghetti | 375 g |
| 1 tbsp | chopped fresh parsley | 15 mL |

● In large skillet, cook pancetta over medium-low heat for about 8 minutes or until crisp; transfer to plate.

● Pour off all but 1 tbsp (15 mL) fat from skillet. Add onion, hot pepper flakes, salt and pepper; cook, stirring occasionally, for 3 minutes.

● Pour in tomatoes; return pancetta to skillet and bring to boil. Reduce heat and simmer for about 10 minutes or until thickened. Stir in half of the Parmesan.

● Meanwhile, in large pot of boiling salted water, cook bucatini for 8 to 10 minutes or until tender but firm; drain well. Toss with sauce; sprinkle with remaining Parmesan and parsley. Makes 4 servings.

**TIP:** Pancetta is rolled bacon that has been cured in salt and spices but has not been smoked. It's available in Italian grocery stores.

*Bucatini, thick tubular spaghetti, is perfect for holding every drop of this classic zesty sauce.*

### WHICH PASTA IS BEST?
● When shopping for pasta, choose a product made from semolina — finely ground granules from the hardest durum wheat. Packages and ingredient lists usually indicate durum semolina or *pasta di semola di grano duro*. This pasta has a pleasant, firm bite to it and will keep its shape when cooked. It is also easier to stuff, and won't soak up excessive amounts of water, sauce or salad dressing.

# Fettuccine with Chicken Livers

*Chicken livers, ground beef, tomatoes and sweet peppers add up to a superlative and inexpensive pasta dish. Since the recipe makes a big batch of sauce, you can divide it into convenient amounts and serve on more than one occasion.*

| | | |
|---|---|---|
| 2 lb | fettuccine | 1 kg |
| 2 tbsp | butter | 25 mL |
| 1 cup | freshly grated Parmesan cheese | 250 mL |
| 1/4 cup | chopped fresh parsley | 50 mL |
| | SAUCE | |
| 1/4 cup | olive oil | 50 mL |
| 1 | clove garlic, minced | 1 |
| 1 lb | lean ground beef | 500 g |
| 1 lb | chicken livers, trimmed and diced | 500 g |
| 1 | can (28 oz/796 mL) tomatoes, puréed | 1 |
| 2 | each sweet green and red peppers, finely chopped | 2 |
| 1 tsp | salt | 5 mL |
| 1/4 tsp | pepper | 1 mL |

● SAUCE: In large deep skillet, heat oil over medium heat; cook garlic and beef, stirring to break up meat, until no longer pink. Add chicken livers; cook until no longer pink.

● Add tomatoes and bring to boil; reduce heat and simmer for about 30 minutes or until reduced and slightly thickened.

● Add green and red peppers, salt and pepper; cook for 15 minutes.

● Meanwhile, in large pot of boiling salted water, cook fettuccine for 8 to 10 minutes or until tender but firm; drain well and toss with butter. Add sauce and mix thoroughly. Stir in cheese and parsley; toss again. Makes 8 to 10 servings.

# Spaghetti with Chicken Livers and Tomatoes

*Chicken livers remain a great bargain, but that's not why you should try this recipe. Try it because the taste is authentically Italian, authentically delicious — and it takes just minutes to make! It's great with a spinach salad.*

| | | |
|---|---|---|
| 2 tbsp | vegetable oil | 25 mL |
| 1 | small onion, chopped | 1 |
| 3 | cloves garlic, finely chopped | 3 |
| Pinch | hot pepper flakes | Pinch |
| 8 oz | chicken livers, trimmed and diced | 250 g |
| 1 | can (28 oz/796 mL) tomatoes, puréed | 1 |
| 1 tsp | each salt and pepper | 5 mL |
| 1 lb | spaghetti | 500 g |
| 2 tbsp | chopped fresh parsley | 25 mL |

● In large deep skillet, heat oil over medium-high heat; cook onion, garlic and hot pepper flakes, stirring occasionally, for 3 to 4 minutes or until softened.

● Add chicken livers and cook until browned. Add tomatoes, salt and pepper; bring to boil. Reduce heat and simmer for 10 minutes or until thickened.

● Meanwhile, in large pot of boiling salted water, cook spaghetti for 8 to 10 minutes or until tender but firm; drain well. Toss with sauce; sprinkle with parsley. Makes 4 servings.

**PASTA STORAGE**

● **Dried pasta** can be stored in an airtight container or package at dry room temperature for up to 1 year.

● **Commercial fresh pasta** should be stored in the refrigerator and used by the "best before" date on the package.

● **Homemade fresh pasta** (see p. 86) is best cooked as soon as it has been made; otherwise, store in refrigerator for up to 2 days.

Or, dry at room temperature and store in refrigerator for up to 1 week.

# Peas, Prosciutto and Tortellini

| | | |
|---|---|---|
| 1 lb | frozen cheese tortellini | 500 g |
| 1 cup | ricotta cheese | 250 mL |
| 3/4 cup | milk | 175 mL |
| 2 tbsp | butter | 25 mL |
| 1/4 cup | chopped green onions | 50 mL |
| 4 | slices prosciutto or ham, chopped | 4 |
| Pinch | hot pepper flakes (optional) | Pinch |
| 2/3 cup | cooked or frozen green peas | 150 mL |
| 1/2 tsp | pepper | 2 mL |
| Pinch | nutmeg | Pinch |
| | Salt | |
| 1/4 cup | freshly grated Parmesan cheese | 50 mL |

● In large pot of boiling salted water, cook tortellini for about 10 minutes or until tender but firm; drain well.

● Meanwhile, in blender or food processor, purée together ricotta cheese and milk until smooth.

● In large skillet, melt butter over medium heat; cook onions, prosciutto, and hot pepper flakes (if using), stirring, for 5 minutes or until softened.

● Stir in cooked tortellini, ricotta mixture, green peas, pepper and nutmeg; cook, stirring, until heated through and tortellini are well coated. Season with salt to taste. Sprinkle with Parmesan. Makes 4 servings.

*Frozen tortellini is the easy answer when you want a satisfying pasta dinner in a hurry. Here, cheese tortellini gets a quick creamy sauce studded with peas.*

# Penne with Sausage and Tomato

| | | |
|---|---|---|
| 12 oz | sweet Italian sausage (about 4) | 375 g |
| 1 tbsp | olive oil | 15 mL |
| 1 | onion, chopped | 1 |
| 1 | sweet red pepper, diced | 1 |
| 1/4 tsp | hot pepper flakes | 1 mL |
| 1 | can (28 oz/796 mL) tomatoes | 1 |
| 1/4 tsp | each salt and pepper | 1 mL |
| 1/4 cup | chopped fresh parsley | 50 mL |
| 4 cups | penne | 1 L |
| | Freshly grated Parmesan cheese | |

● Remove casings from sausage; crumble meat. In large skillet, heat oil over medium-high heat; cook sausage, onion, red pepper and hot pepper flakes, stirring, for 5 minutes or until sausage is no longer pink.

● Drain and chop tomatoes, reserving 1/4 cup (50 mL) juice. Add tomatoes, juice, salt and pepper to skillet; bring to boil. Reduce heat and simmer for 5 to 7 minutes or until slightly thickened. Stir in parsley.

● Meanwhile, in large pot of boiling salted water, cook penne for 8 to 10 minutes or until tender but firm; drain well. Toss with sauce; sprinkle with Parmesan to taste. Makes 4 servings.

*When you're looking for an ingredient that gives you flavor fast, you'll find sausage comes to the rescue quite often. Naturally, the better the sausage, the better the sauce — so it's worth finding the best maker of fresh sausages in your community.*

# Spaghetti Carbonara

*This satisfying combo of bacon (pancetta), eggs and creamy cheese cloaking strands of spaghetti is just the dish to have in your repertoire when (a) the cupboard is pretty bare, (b) you don't have a lot of time, and (c) you and your household need a comforting dish. A green salad is nice alongside.*

| 2 tbsp | butter or olive oil | 25 mL |
|---|---|---|
| 1 | onion, chopped | 1 |
| 2 | cloves garlic, minced | 2 |
| 4 oz | pancetta or bacon, diced | 125 g |
| 3 | eggs | 3 |
| 1 tsp | salt | 5 mL |
| 12 oz | spaghetti | 375 g |
| 1/2 cup | freshly grated Parmesan cheese | 125 mL |
| 2 tbsp | chopped fresh parsley | 25 mL |

● In small skillet, melt butter over medium heat; cook onion and garlic for 3 minutes or until softened. Add pancetta; cook, stirring occasionally, for about 6 minutes or until slightly crisp.

● In small bowl, lightly beat eggs with salt; set aside.

● Meanwhile, in large pot of boiling salted water, cook spaghetti for 8 to 10 minutes or until tender but firm. Drain and return to pot over medium heat.

● Immediately stir in Parmesan, parsley and pancetta mixture. Stir in eggs; cook, stirring, for about 30 seconds or until eggs are lightly cooked and pasta is coated. Serve immediately. Makes 4 servings.

# Farfalle with Ham and Ricotta

*Pasta bows show off a creamy sauce flecked with green onion and ham.*

| 6 oz | thinly sliced Black Forest ham | 175 g |
|---|---|---|
| 1 | stalk celery | 1 |
| 5 | green onions | 5 |
| 1 tbsp | butter | 15 mL |
| 2 cups | ricotta cheese | 500 mL |
| 2 tbsp | milk | 25 mL |
| 1/4 tsp | dried sage | 1 mL |
| Pinch | nutmeg | Pinch |
| 1/2 cup | freshly grated Parmesan cheese | 125 mL |
| | Salt and pepper | |
| 6 cups | farfalle | 1.5 L |

● Slice ham and celery into thin strips, about 1-1/2 inches (4 cm) long and 1/4 inch (5 mm) wide. Cut onions in half lengthwise; cut into 1-1/2-inch (4 cm) long strips.

● In skillet, melt butter over medium-high heat; cook ham, celery and onions, stirring occasionally, for 5 to 7 minutes or until vegetables are softened and just beginning to brown.

● Add ricotta, milk, sage and nutmeg; reduce heat to medium-low and cook, stirring, until warmed through (cheese will still appear curdy). Stir in Parmesan, and salt and pepper to taste.

● Meanwhile, in large pot of boiling salted water, cook farfalle for 8 to 10 minutes or until tender but firm; drain well. Toss with sauce. Makes 4 servings.

**TIP:** Avoid powdered sage since it gives a fusty, tired taste to any dish it touches. Instead, dry your own bunches of fresh sage and crumble for sauces like this one, or buy crumbled sage in bottles at the supermarket.

# Shrimp and Vegetable Pasta  ▲

| | | |
|---|---|---|
| 3/4 cup | chicken stock | 175 mL |
| 1 | onion, chopped | 1 |
| 1 | carrot, thinly sliced | 1 |
| 3 | cloves garlic, minced | 3 |
| 1/4 tsp | each salt and pepper | 1 mL |
| 6 oz | large shrimp, peeled and deveined | 175 g |
| 2 cups | broccoli florets | 500 mL |
| 1 | sweet red pepper, diced | 1 |
| 2 tbsp | chopped fresh dill | 25 mL |
| 1 tsp | Worcestershire sauce | 5 mL |
| 4 oz | linguine or spaghetti | 125 g |
| 1/3 cup | freshly grated Parmesan cheese | 75 mL |

● In skillet, bring stock to boil; add onion, carrot, garlic, salt and pepper. Reduce heat and simmer for 5 minutes.

● Add shrimp, broccoli and red pepper; return to boil. Reduce heat and simmer, covered, for 3 to 5 minutes or until shrimp are pink and broccoli is tender-crisp. Stir in dill and Worcestershire sauce.

● Meanwhile, in pot of boiling salted water, cook linguine for 8 to 10 minutes or until tender but firm; drain well. Arrange on plates; sprinkle with half of the Parmesan. Top with shrimp mixture; sprinkle with remaining Parmesan. Makes 2 servings.

P*asta is a wonderful solution when serving one or two. Cooking the toppings all together also cuts out mess and fuss.*

# Capellini with Smoked Salmon and Lemon Cream Sauce

*There's no fooling this time. Whipping cream is at the heart of this lemon-accented sauce — a whole cupful (250 mL)! — and it's definitely a special-occasion dish. (See photo, p. 4.)*

| | | |
|---|---|---|
| 1 cup | whipping cream | 250 mL |
| 1 tsp | grated lemon rind | 5 mL |
| 1/2 tsp | salt | 2 mL |
| 1/4 tsp | white pepper | 1 mL |
| 6 oz | smoked salmon, cut into 1/2-inch (1 cm) wide strips | 175 g |
| 1 cup | frozen peas | 250 mL |
| 12 oz | capellini or spaghettini | 375 g |
| 2 tbsp | butter | 25 mL |
| 2 tbsp | lemon juice | 25 mL |
| 2 tbsp | chopped green onion | 25 mL |

● In saucepan, bring cream to boil; stir in lemon rind, salt and pepper. Reduce heat and simmer gently, stirring occasionally, for 5 minutes or until thickened slightly. Stir in salmon and peas; cook for 1 minute.

● Meanwhile, in large pot of boiling salted water, cook capellini for 6 to 8 minutes or until tender but firm; drain well. Toss with butter, lemon juice and sauce. Sprinkle with green onion. Makes 4 servings.

# Easy Tuna and Garlic Pasta

*This is a gutsy pasta, probably more for adults than kids, and ideal for a quick supper. If time is short, use thawed frozen spinach, making sure all the excess liquid is pressed out before chopping. Pasta shells (conchiglie) catch the chunky sauce nicely.*

| | | |
|---|---|---|
| 1 | pkg (10 oz/284 g) fresh spinach, trimmed | 1 |
| 1/4 cup | extra virgin olive oil | 50 mL |
| 1 | onion, chopped | 1 |
| 4 | cloves garlic, minced | 4 |
| 1/3 cup | chopped fresh basil or parsley | 75 mL |
| 1 tsp | each salt and pepper | 5 mL |
| 4 cups | conchiglie or rotini | 1 L |
| 2 | cans (each 7-1/2 oz/213 mL) tuna, drained and broken into chunks | 2 |

● Rinse spinach; shake off excess water. In saucepan, cook spinach, with just the water clinging to leaves, over high heat for 1 to 2 minutes or until wilted. Drain and let cool slightly; squeeze out excess liquid. Chop coarsely and set aside.

● In skillet, heat oil over medium-low heat; cook onion and garlic for 5 minutes or until softened. Add spinach, basil, salt and pepper; cook, stirring, for 2 minutes or until heated through.

● Meanwhile, in large pot of boiling salted water, cook conchiglie for 8 to 10 minutes or until tender but firm; drain well. Lightly toss with spinach mixture, then tuna. Makes 4 servings.

## BUYING AND PREPARING MUSSELS

● Mussels must be alive when purchased. Gathered wild mussels have shells that are tightly closed, but the shells of cultivated mussels, the kind now most available at fish counters, tend to gape. Test each mussel individually, tapping it lightly. Alive mussels close up quickly. Those that remain open should be avoided.

● Just to be sure, hold each closed mussel between your thumb and forefinger, pressing the shells gently on the bias. If the shell opens, the mussel is dead.

● To keep mussels alive until cooking time, transfer them as soon as possible from store wrappings to bowl. Cover with wet cloth and store in refrigerator. Do not cover mussels with water.

● As close as possible to cooking time, scrub mussels with a stiff brush under cold running water. Pull beard back while cutting it off with a knife or mussel shell.

# Fusilli with Mussels ▲

| 2 lb | mussels | 1 kg |
|---|---|---|
| 2 tbsp | olive oil | 25 mL |
| 1 | onion, chopped | 1 |
| 4 | cloves garlic, thinly sliced | 4 |
| 1 cup | clam juice | 250 mL |
| 1 tsp | dried thyme | 5 mL |
| 1/4 tsp | hot pepper sauce | 1 mL |
| 1 | can (19 oz/540 mL) tomatoes, drained and chopped | 1 |
| 2 tbsp | butter | 25 mL |
| 1/3 cup | chopped fresh parsley | 75 mL |
|  | Salt and pepper |  |
| 1 lb | fusilli lunghi, linguine or spaghetti | 500 g |

● Scrub mussels under running water and remove any beards; discard any that do not close when tapped.

● In large saucepan, heat oil over high heat; cook onion and garlic for 2 minutes or until softened. Stir in clam juice, thyme, hot pepper sauce and tomatoes; bring to boil.

● Add mussels; cover and steam for 3 minutes. Remove mussels as they open; keep warm. Discard any that do not open.

● Cook sauce over high heat for 5 to 6 minutes or until reduced to 2-1/2 cups (625 mL). Stir in butter until melted; stir in half of the parsley. Season with salt and pepper to taste.

● Meanwhile, in large pot of boiling salted water, cook fusilli for 8 to 10 minutes or until tender but firm; drain well and toss with sauce. Arrange in center of warmed serving platter. Garnish with reserved mussels and remaining parsley. Makes 4 servings.

*For an impressive platter, toss long fusilli with the sauce and surround it with mussels. If you like, remove some of the mussels from their shells while the sauce is reducing and toss them with the pasta and sauce.*

# Creamy Scallop Linguine with Vegetables ◄

| | | |
|---|---|---|
| 2 tbsp | butter | 25 mL |
| 1 | onion, finely chopped | 1 |
| 1 | clove garlic, minced | 1 |
| 3 cups | thickly sliced mushrooms (12 oz/375 g) | 750 mL |
| 2 | stalks celery, julienned | 2 |
| 2 | carrots or 1 sweet red pepper, julienned | 2 |
| 2 tbsp | all-purpose flour | 25 mL |
| 3/4 cup | clam juice, fish stock or chicken stock | 175 mL |
| 1 cup | light cream | 250 mL |
| 1/2 tsp | salt | 2 mL |
| 1/4 tsp | pepper | 1 mL |
| 1 lb | scallops, halved if large | 500 g |
| 1 tsp | Pernod (optional) | 5 mL |
| 1 lb | linguine | 500 g |

● In skillet or heavy saucepan, melt butter over medium heat; cook onion and garlic for about 3 minutes or until softened. Add mushrooms; cook, stirring occasionally, for 5 minutes. Stir in celery and carrots; cook, stirring occasionally, until tender-crisp.

● Sprinkle with flour; cook, stirring, for 1 minute. Pour in clam juice; bring to boil, stirring constantly. Whisk in cream, salt and pepper but do not boil.

● Add scallops; cook for 3 to 4 minutes or just until opaque. (Do not overcook or scallops will be tough.) Stir in Pernod (if using).

● Meanwhile, in large pot of boiling salted water, cook linguine for 8 to 10 minutes or until tender but firm; drain well. Gently toss with sauce. Makes 4 main-course or 8 appetizer servings.

*Entertaining with pasta calls for a special sauce, and this creamy one, studded with scallops, suits cooking for company perfectly.*

# Seafood Fettuccine

| | | |
|---|---|---|
| 1 tbsp | olive oil | 15 mL |
| 1 | onion, chopped | 1 |
| 2 | cloves garlic, chopped | 2 |
| 1 tsp | dried oregano | 5 mL |
| Pinch | hot pepper flakes | Pinch |
| 1 | can (19 oz/540 mL) tomatoes, puréed | 1 |
| 1 tsp | salt | 5 mL |
| 1/2 tsp | pepper | 2 mL |
| 1/4 cup | whipping cream | 50 mL |
| 6 oz | mussels (see sidebar, p. 32) | 175 g |
| 8 oz | deveined peeled shrimp | 250 g |
| 8 oz | scallops | 250 g |
| 12 oz | fettuccine or linguine | 375 g |
| 1/4 cup | chopped fresh parsley | 50 mL |

● In large saucepan, heat oil over medium heat; cook onion, garlic, oregano and hot pepper flakes, stirring, for 3 minutes or until softened.

● Stir in tomatoes, salt and pepper; bring to boil. Reduce heat and simmer for 15 to 20 minutes or until thickened. Stir in cream; simmer for 5 minutes.

● Meanwhile, scrub mussels under running water and remove any beards; discard any that do not close when tapped. Add to saucepan along with shrimp and scallops; cover and cook for 5 minutes or just until scallops are opaque, shrimp are pink and mussels have opened. Discard any mussels that do not open.

● Meanwhile, in large pot of boiling salted water, cook fettuccine until tender but firm; drain well. Toss with sauce; sprinkle with parsley. Makes 4 servings.

*This special little dinner for friends also makes a gorgeous appetizer for eight.*

# Spaghetti with Fast Clam and Garlic Sauce

*It's worth keeping a few cans of baby clams on hand to whip up this zesty dish for unexpected company.*

| | | |
|---|---|---|
| 1/4 cup | butter | 50 mL |
| 1 | small onion, chopped | 1 |
| 4 | cloves garlic, minced | 4 |
| 1/3 cup | (approx) chopped fresh parsley | 75 mL |
| 2 | cans (each 5 oz/142 g) baby clams | 2 |
| 1/4 cup | dry vermouth or clam juice | 50 mL |
| 1/4 tsp | each salt and pepper | 1 mL |
| Pinch | hot pepper flakes | Pinch |
| 12 oz | spaghetti | 375 g |

● In skillet, melt butter over medium heat; cook onion, garlic and parsley, stirring, for about 3 minutes or until softened.

● Drain clams, adding liquid to skillet. Add vermouth, salt, pepper and hot pepper flakes; cook for 5 to 8 minutes or until reduced by half. Add clams; cook for 1 minute.

● Meanwhile, in pot of boiling salted water, cook spaghetti for 8 to 10 minutes or until tender but firm; drain well. Toss with sauce; sprinkle with more parsley. Makes 4 servings.

# Rotini with Broccoli and Clams

*Purists don't serve Parmesan with seafood sauces — but with clams, the cheese does add an enjoyable finish.*

| | | |
|---|---|---|
| 1-1/3 cups | rotini | 325 mL |
| 2 cups | broccoli florets | 500 mL |
| 1 tbsp | each butter and olive oil | 15 mL |
| 2 | cloves garlic, minced | 2 |
| Pinch | hot pepper flakes | Pinch |
| 1 | can (5 oz/142 g) baby clams | 1 |
| | Pepper | |
| 1/4 cup | freshly grated Parmesan cheese | 50 mL |

● In large pot of boiling salted water, cook rotini for 6 minutes. Add broccoli; cook for about 2 minutes or until pasta is tender but firm. Drain well.

● Meanwhile, in large skillet, melt butter with oil over low heat; cook garlic and hot pepper flakes, stirring, for 3 minutes. Drain clams, reserving liquid. Add clams to skillet; cook until heated through. Stir in liquid.

● Add pasta mixture and increase heat to high; cook, stirring often, for about 4 minutes or until most of the liquid is absorbed. Sprinkle with pepper to taste and Parmesan. Makes 2 servings.

## STOCKING THE CUPBOARD FOR PASTA

*Yikes, the fridge is bare! Don't worry, though. If your cupboard is strategically stocked with the following never-be-without ingredients, you'll always be able to toss up a satisfying pasta dish in no time at all:*

● tomato-based pasta sauces (include ones fortified with vegetables, mushrooms, herbs and meat)

● cans of tomatoes, tomato sauce and tomato paste
● mushrooms
● sun-dried tomatoes

● dried mushrooms
● olives
● olive oil, including extra virgin
● canned clams, tuna, salmon and anchovies

● evaporated milk
● chicken stock
● chick-peas
● onions and garlic
● dried herbs, especially basil

● hot pepper flakes
● roasted red peppers in jars
● and pasta, of course, in all your favorite shapes and sizes.

# Tomato Clam Pasta ▲

| | | |
|---|---|---|
| 1 tbsp | olive oil | 15 mL |
| 1 | large onion, chopped | 1 |
| 3 | cloves garlic, minced | 3 |
| 1 | can (28 oz/796 mL) stewed tomatoes | 1 |
| 3 tbsp | tomato paste | 50 mL |
| 1 | can (5 oz/142 g) baby clams | 1 |
| 1/2 tsp | dried oregano | 2 mL |
| Pinch | hot pepper flakes | Pinch |
| 1 tsp | dried parsley | 5 mL |
| | Salt and pepper | |
| 4 cups | rotini | 1 L |
| 1/2 cup | freshly grated Parmesan cheese | 125 mL |

● In heavy saucepan, heat oil over medium heat; cook onion and garlic, stirring, for about 5 minutes or until softened. Add tomatoes, crushing with fork; stir in tomato paste.

● Drain clams, pouring juice into saucepan; set clams aside. Stir in oregano and hot pepper flakes; bring to boil. Reduce heat and simmer for 30 minutes or until thickened. Add clams, parsley, and salt and pepper to taste; heat through.

● Meanwhile, in large pot of boiling salted water, cook rotini for 6 to 8 minutes or until tender but firm; drain well. Toss with sauce; sprinkle with Parmesan. Makes 4 servings.

*For extra color, add zucchini and carrots to the onions while they cook.*

# Spinach Fettuccine with Cauliflower and Anchovy Sauce ▲

The rich flavors of olive oil, garlic and anchovies blend subtly with cauliflower and Parmesan cheese to make a delightful, almost creamy, sauce.

| | | |
|---|---|---|
| 12 oz | spinach fettuccine | 375 g |
| 4 cups | cauliflower florets (about half a head) | 1 L |
| 3 tbsp | extra virgin olive oil | 50 mL |
| 1 | clove garlic, minced | 1 |
| 4 | anchovy fillets, minced (or 2 tsp/10 mL anchovy paste) | 4 |
| 2 tbsp | butter | 25 mL |
| 1/3 cup | freshly grated Parmesan cheese | 75 mL |
| | Pepper | |

● In large pot of boiling salted water, cook fettuccine for 8 to 10 minutes or until tender but firm; drain well.

● Meanwhile, steam cauliflower for about 3 minutes or until tender-crisp.

● In large skillet, heat oil over medium heat; cook garlic for 1 minute. Add anchovies; cook, stirring, for 2 minutes.

● Toss cauliflower, anchovies and butter with fettuccine. Add Parmesan, and pepper to taste; toss again. Makes 4 servings.

# Penne with Anchovy Tomato Sauce

| 1 tbsp | olive oil | 15 mL |
|---|---|---|
| 3 | cloves garlic, minced | 3 |
| 1/4 tsp | hot pepper flakes | 1 mL |
| 3 | anchovies, chopped | 3 |
| 1 | can (28 oz/796 mL) tomatoes, drained | 1 |
| 1/4 cup | chopped fresh parsley | 50 mL |
| 1/4 tsp | each salt and pepper | 1 mL |
| 5 cups | penne or fusilli | 1.25 L |

● In skillet, heat oil over low heat; cook garlic and hot pepper flakes for 3 minutes or until garlic is softened but not browned. Add anchovies; cook for 1 minute.

● Increase heat to medium-high. Add tomatoes, breaking up with spoon; cook, stirring occasionally, for 5 minutes or until thickened slightly. Stir in parsley, salt and pepper.

● Meanwhile, in large pot of boiling salted water, cook penne for 8 to 10 minutes or until tender but firm; drain well. Toss with sauce. Makes 4 servings.

*If you're the kind of person who always says, "Hold the anchovies," this recipe may make you change your mind! Once cooked, there is only the mellowest hint of them in the flavorful sauce.*

# Spaghetti with Anchovies, Walnuts and Garlic

| 2 | cans (2 oz/50 g) anchovy fillets (packed in oil) | 2 |
|---|---|---|
| 1/2 cup | extra virgin olive oil | 125 mL |
| 8 | cloves garlic, minced | 8 |
| 12 oz | spaghetti or vermicelli | 375 g |
| 1/2 cup | walnuts, finely chopped | 125 mL |
| 1/3 cup | chopped fresh parsley | 75 mL |

● Drain anchovies; rinse under cold water. Pat dry and chop.

● In large skillet, heat oil over low heat; cook garlic and anchovies, stirring occasionally, for about 15 minutes or until garlic is lightly golden.

● Meanwhile, in large pot of boiling salted water, cook spaghetti for 8 to 10 minutes or until tender but firm; drain well. Toss with sauce, walnuts and parsley. Makes 4 servings.

*Anchovies full steam ahead with garlic and a simple toss of spaghetti. This unusual little sauce is just right for a small dinner party starter.*

# Linguine with Salmon and Dill

| 1 cup | ricotta cheese | 250 mL |
|---|---|---|
| 3/4 cup | milk | 175 mL |
| 2 tbsp | butter | 25 mL |
| 1 | clove garlic, minced | 1 |
| 4 | green onions, finely chopped | 4 |
| 1 tbsp | chopped fresh dill (or 1 tsp/5 mL dried dillweed) | 15 mL |
| 6 oz | smoked salmon, cut into strips | 175 g |
| 12 oz | linguine or spaghetti | 375 g |
| 1/2 tsp | pepper | 2 mL |
| 1/4 cup | freshly grated Parmesan cheese (optional) | 50 mL |

● In food processor or blender, purée together ricotta and milk until smooth; set aside.

● In skillet, melt butter over medium heat; cook garlic, onions and dill, stirring, for about 3 minutes or until softened. Add salmon and ricotta mixture; cook over low heat for about 3 minutes or until heated through.

● Meanwhile, in large pot of boiling salted water, cook linguine for 8 to 10 minutes or until tender but firm; drain well. Toss with sauce; sprinkle with pepper, and Parmesan (if using). Makes 4 servings.

*All you need is a little smoked salmon to flavor this delightful pasta dish. The surprise is that it's not cream that gives the sauce its wonderful texture — it's a puréed blend of milk and ricotta cheese.*

# Wok, Pot and Skillet

From trendy stir-fried Pad Thai to easy frittata in a skillet
or minestrone by the bowl, pasta is the versatile star of all these
dishes — and more!

## Minestrone Warm-Up ▶

*You don't have to speak Italian to know that "minestrone" translates into a nourishing bean and pasta soup chock-full of flavor and satisfaction.*

| | | |
|---|---|---|
| 1 cup | dried red or white kidney beans | 250 mL |
| 1 tbsp | olive oil | 15 mL |
| 4 oz | pancetta or bacon (unsliced), cubed | 125 g |
| 2 | cloves garlic, minced | 2 |
| 2 | onions, chopped | 2 |
| 8 cups | chicken stock | 2 L |
| 2 | each carrots and stalks celery, diagonally sliced | 2 |
| Half | small cabbage, shredded | Half |
| 1 | can (28 oz/796 mL) tomatoes, mashed | 1 |
| 1 | bay leaf | 1 |
| 1 tsp | each dried basil and oregano | 5 mL |
| 1/2 tsp | salt | 2 mL |
| 1/4 tsp | pepper | 1 mL |
| 3 | potatoes, peeled and cubed | 3 |
| 1 cup | rotini, macaroni or tubetti | 250 mL |
| | **PARSLEY PESTO** | |
| 1 cup | packed fresh parsley | 250 mL |
| 1/4 cup | extra virgin olive oil | 50 mL |
| 2 tbsp | pine nuts or walnuts | 25 mL |
| 1 | clove garlic, minced | 1 |

| | | |
|---|---|---|
| 1/4 cup | freshly grated Parmesan cheese | 50 mL |
| | Salt and pepper | |

● In bowl, cover beans with 3 cups (750 mL) water. Cover and soak overnight; drain, discarding water.

● In Dutch oven, heat oil over medium-high heat; cook pancetta, garlic and onions for 5 minutes or until softened.

● Add beans and stock; bring to boil, skimming off foam. Cover and simmer over medium-low heat for 1 hour or until beans are tender.

● Add carrots, celery, cabbage, tomatoes, bay leaf, basil, oregano, salt and pepper; bring to boil. Reduce heat, cover and simmer for 20 minutes. Add potatoes and rotini; simmer, covered, for 10 to 15 minutes or until potatoes are tender. Discard bay leaf.

● PARSLEY PESTO: Meanwhile, in food processor, purée parsley, oil and pine nuts until smooth; transfer to bowl. Stir in garlic and Parmesan. Season with salt and pepper to taste.

● Ladle soup into bowls; top each with 1 tbsp (15 mL) pesto. Makes 8 servings.

**TIP:** You can make the soup ahead of time and refrigerate it for up to 5 days. To freeze it for up to 1 month, omit the potatoes and pasta. Add them when reheating by simmering, covered, for 10 to 15 minutes or until potatoes are tender, adding more chicken stock if desired.

# Speedy Tomato, Chick-Pea and Spinach Soup ▶

*J anuary cold holds no threat when you come home to this chunky soup. Grate or shave a little cheese over the top and serve with whole grain bread or focaccia.*

| | | |
|---|---|---|
| 2 cups | vegetable stock | 500 mL |
| 1 | can (28 oz/796 mL) tomatoes | 1 |
| 1 | onion, chopped | 1 |
| 1 | clove garlic, minced | 1 |
| 1/4 tsp | dried sage | 1 mL |
| 1 cup | rotini | 250 mL |
| 1 | can (19 oz/540 mL) chick-peas, drained and rinsed | 1 |
| 2 cups | chopped fresh spinach | 500 mL |
| 1/4 tsp | pepper | 1 mL |
| Dash | hot pepper sauce | Dash |

● In large saucepan, combine stock and tomatoes, breaking up with fork. Add onion, garlic and sage; bring to boil. Add rotini and reduce heat to medium-low; cover and simmer for 7 minutes.

● Add chick-peas and spinach; cover and cook for 3 minutes or until pasta is tender but firm. Stir in pepper and hot pepper sauce. Makes 4 to 6 servings.

# Starry Stracciatella

*T his chicken-broth-and-swirled-egg soup spells instant supper. The pasta stars (stellini) and peas add substance.*

| | | |
|---|---|---|
| 2 | cans (each 10 oz/284 mL) chicken broth | 2 |
| 1/2 cup | stellini | 125 mL |
| 1 cup | frozen peas | 250 mL |
| 1 | egg | 1 |
| 1/3 cup | freshly grated Parmesan cheese | 75 mL |

● In saucepan, bring broth and 3-1/2 cups (875 mL) water to boil. Stir in stellini; cook for 3 minutes. Add peas; cook for 2 minutes or until pasta is tender but firm.

● In bowl and using fork, beat egg; gradually pour into broth mixture, stirring with fork to keep mixture stringy. Serve sprinkled with Parmesan. Makes 6 servings.

# Oriental Shrimp Noodle Soup ▶

*F or extra flavor, add a splash of sherry to the soup just before serving.*

| | | |
|---|---|---|
| 2 tsp | vegetable oil | 10 mL |
| 1 | onion, chopped | 1 |
| 2 | cloves garlic, minced | 2 |
| 1 tbsp | minced gingerroot | 15 mL |
| Pinch | hot pepper flakes (optional) | Pinch |
| 8 cups | chicken stock | 2 L |
| 1 cup | each diagonally sliced carrot and celery | 250 mL |
| 2 cups | snow peas, halved | 500 mL |
| 12 oz | shrimp, peeled and deveined | 375 g |
| 4 oz | rice vermicelli | 125 g |
| 2 tbsp | soy sauce | 25 mL |
| 1/4 tsp | pepper | 1 mL |

● In Dutch oven or large saucepan, heat oil over medium heat; cook onion, garlic, ginger, and hot pepper flakes (if using) for 3 minutes or until softened.

● Add stock, carrot and celery; bring to boil. Reduce heat to medium-low; cover and simmer for 5 minutes. Add snow peas and shrimp; simmer, covered, for 3 minutes.

● Break vermicelli into 2-inch (5 cm) pieces and add to soup; cover and simmer for 2 to 3 minutes or until vegetables are tender and shrimp are pink. Stir in soy sauce and pepper. Makes 5 to 7 servings.

# Cheesy Pasta Frittata ▼

*This easy meal-in-a-skillet is one the whole family will enjoy. In season, take advantage of fresh peas and corn. Any short pasta, such as penne or macaroni, can be used.*

| | | |
|---|---|---|
| 1 cup | fusilli | 250 mL |
| 1 tbsp | butter | 15 mL |
| 1 tbsp | olive oil | 15 mL |
| 1 | onion, chopped | 1 |
| 1/2 cup | sliced mushrooms | 125 mL |
| 1/2 cup | corn kernels | 125 mL |
| 1/2 cup | peas | 125 mL |
| 8 | eggs | 8 |
| 1/2 cup | shredded Cheddar cheese | 125 mL |
| 1/2 tsp | salt | 2 mL |
| 1/4 tsp | pepper | 1 mL |
| | SALSA | |
| 2 cups | chopped seeded tomatoes | 500 mL |
| 1 tbsp | chopped fresh basil | 15 mL |
| 1 tsp | olive oil | 5 mL |
| 1 | clove garlic, minced | 1 |
| Dash | hot pepper sauce | Dash |
| | Salt and pepper | |

● In large pot of boiling salted water, cook fusilli for 8 to 10 minutes or until tender but firm; drain well.

● Salsa: Meanwhile, combine tomatoes, basil, oil, garlic, hot pepper sauce, and salt and pepper to taste; set aside.

● In 9-inch (23 cm) ovenproof skillet, heat butter and oil over medium heat; cook onion and mushrooms for 3 minutes or until tender. Add fusilli, corn and peas; toss to mix well.

● Whisk together eggs, cheese, salt and pepper; pour into skillet.

● Cook for 5 to 8 minutes or until bottom is set. Bake in 350°F (180°C) oven for 5 to 7 minutes or until slightly puffy and set in center but still moist. Cut frittata into wedges; serve with salsa. Makes 6 servings.

# Spaghetti Frittata

| 8 oz | spaghetti | 250 g |
|---|---|---|
| 1/3 cup | freshly grated Parmesan cheese | 75 mL |
| 1/4 cup | butter | 50 mL |
| 2 tbsp | chopped fresh parsley | 25 mL |
| 4 | eggs | 4 |
| 1/2 tsp | each salt and pepper | 2 mL |

● In large pot of boiling salted water, cook spaghetti for 8 to 10 minutes or until tender but firm; drain well. Transfer to bowl. Stir in cheese, 3 tbsp (50 mL) of the butter and parsley; let cool slightly.

● Beat together eggs, salt and pepper; add to spaghetti mixture, mixing well.

● In large nonstick skillet, heat remaining butter over medium heat until foaming; pour in spaghetti mixture and spread evenly. Cook for 4 to 5 minutes or until bottom is golden brown.

● Loosen frittata with spatula; invert onto plate. Slide frittata back into skillet and cook for 3 to 4 minutes or until bottom is golden brown. Cut into wedges to serve. Makes 4 servings.

*This Italian-style omelette makes a quick low-cost dinner and is a great way to use up leftover pasta.*

# Mexican-Style Pork Chop and Spaghetti Bake

| 3 tbsp | vegetable oil | 50 mL |
|---|---|---|
| 1 | onion, chopped | 1 |
| 2 | cloves garlic, minced | 2 |
| 1 | can (19 oz/540 mL) tomatoes | 1 |
| 1 | can (4 oz/114 mL) diced green chilies, drained and rinsed | 1 |
| 1 tbsp | chopped fresh parsley | 15 mL |
| 2 tsp | chili powder | 10 mL |
| 1 tsp | ground cumin | 5 mL |
| 1/2 tsp | dried oregano | 2 mL |
| 4 cups | boiling water | 1 L |
| 8 oz | spaghetti, broken in half | 250 g |
| 4 | pork chops | 4 |
| Pinch | each salt and pepper | Pinch |
| 3/4 cup | shredded Cheddar cheese | 175 mL |
| | Parsley sprigs | |

● In large saucepan, heat 2 tbsp (25 mL) of the oil over medium heat; cook onion and garlic for 3 minutes or until softened.

● Add tomatoes, breaking up with fork. Stir in green chilies, parsley, chili powder, cumin and oregano. Stir in boiling water and bring to boil; add spaghetti. Reduce heat to medium-low; cover and simmer, stirring occasionally, for 20 to 25 minutes or until most of the liquid has been absorbed.

● Meanwhile, trim fat from chops. In large ovenproof skillet, heat remaining oil over medium-high heat; cook chops, without turning, for 10 minutes. Turn chops over and sprinkle with salt and pepper; cover and cook for 5 minutes longer or just until no longer pink inside but still moist.

● Remove chops from skillet and drain off any fat. Spread spaghetti mixture in skillet; top with chops. *(Recipe can be prepared to this point, cooled, covered and refrigerated for up to 6 hours. Heat in 350°F/180°C oven for 20 minutes before continuing.)*

● Sprinkle cheese over chops; bake in 350°F (180°C) oven for 5 to 10 minutes or until cheese melts. Garnish with parsley. Makes 4 servings.

*This easy pork chop and pasta skillet supper is perfect any day of the week. Serve it right away or make it ahead of time for a satisfying no-fuss meal in minutes.*

# Pad Thai ◄

| | | |
|---|---|---:|
| 1 | pkg (227 g) wide rice stick noodles | 1 |
| 1/2 cup | chicken stock | 125 mL |
| 1/4 cup | granulated sugar | 50 mL |
| 1/4 cup | fish sauce | 50 mL |
| 3 tbsp | lime juice | 45 mL |
| 2 tbsp | ketchup | 25 mL |
| 1/4 tsp | hot pepper flakes | 1 mL |
| 4 oz | boneless pork loin | 125 g |
| 6 oz | firm tofu | 175 g |
| 1/4 cup | vegetable oil | 50 mL |
| 1 | egg, beaten | 1 |
| 3 | cloves garlic, minced | 3 |
| 8 oz | large raw shrimp, peeled and deveined | 250 g |
| 1 | sweet red pepper, diced | 1 |
| 2 cups | bean sprouts | 500 mL |
| 1/2 cup | coriander leaves, coarsely chopped | 125 mL |
| 6 | green onions, thinly sliced | 6 |
| 1/4 cup | unsalted peanuts, chopped | 50 mL |

● In large bowl, soak noodles in warm water for 15 minutes; drain and set aside.

● Meanwhile, in small bowl, whisk together chicken stock, sugar, fish sauce, lime juice, ketchup and hot pepper flakes; set sauce aside.

● Cut pork across the grain into 1/4-inch (5 mm) thick strips. Cut tofu into 1/2-inch (1 cm) cubes. Set aside.

● In wok or large skillet, heat 1 tsp (5 mL) of the oil over medium heat; cook egg, stirring occasionally, for about 3 minutes or until scrambled and set. Transfer to large plate.

● Wipe out wok; add 1 tbsp (15 mL) of the oil. Increase heat to medium-high; stir-fry garlic, shrimp and pork for about 3 minutes or until shrimp are bright pink. Add to egg.

● Heat remaining oil in pan. Stir in tofu and red pepper; cook, stirring occasionally, for 2 minutes or until tofu begins to brown. Gently stir in noodles for 1 minute or until beginning to wilt. Pour in sauce; stir-fry for 3 minutes or until noodles are tender.

● Return egg mixture to pan; add bean sprouts, coriander and half of the green onions. Stir-fry for 2 to 3 minutes or until heated through. Remove to warmed serving platter; garnish with peanuts and remaining green onions. Makes 4 servings.

*This supper-size stir-fried noodle salad from Thailand is a symphony of flavors and textures. The lilt of fresh coriander and lime plays along with assertive garlic, sweet shrimp, salty fish sauce and crunchy bean sprouts.*

**TIPS:**

● Soaking times for rice noodles are important because the noodles absorb liquid as long as they are in it and can become too soft and swollen.

● For a change of taste, substitute a 4 oz (125 g) boneless skinless chicken breast for the pork. If rice noodles are unavailable, 12 oz (375 g) fettuccine, cooked, can be stirred into the wok after the tofu.

**THAI INGREDIENTS**

**Coriander**, often known by its Spanish translation, cilantro, is the soul of Thai food, here adding a punch of its aromatic funky flavor right at the very end.

**Fish Sauce** is a clear amber-colored sauce, either shrimp- or anchovy-flavored, used extensively in Southeast Asian cooking to provide saltiness and to enhance the taste of other ingredients. Store opened bottle in refrigerator.

# Skillet Turkey and Pasta Supper

*When there's not much time, this satisfying one-pot supper is sure to please. Made with turkey and no added fat, it's a lean and tasty update of the old hamburger pasta supper.*

| | | |
|---|---|---|
| 12 oz | ground turkey | 375 g |
| 1 | onion, chopped | 1 |
| 1 | sweet green pepper, chopped | 1 |
| 1 | clove garlic, minced | 1 |
| 1/2 tsp | each dried thyme and salt | 2 mL |
| 1/4 tsp | pepper | 1 mL |
| 1 | can (28 oz/796 mL) stewed tomatoes | 1 |
| 2 tbsp | tomato paste | 25 mL |
| 1-1/2 cups | rotini | 375 mL |

● In large nonstick skillet, cook turkey over high heat, stirring often, for 3 to 5 minutes or until no longer pink. Drain off any fat.

● Add onion, green pepper, garlic, thyme, salt and pepper; cook, stirring, for 3 minutes. Add tomatoes, breaking up with spoon. Add tomato paste and 1/2 cup (125 mL) water; bring to boil.

● Add rotini and reduce heat to low; partially cover and cook, stirring often, for 20 to 25 minutes or until thickened and pasta is tender but firm. Makes 4 servings.

# Sesame Tofu and Vegetable Stir-Fry ▶

*Tofu is the chameleon of cooking, taking on the flavors of companion ingredients. In this one-dish supper, the flavor it drinks up is the classic Oriental soy sauce and sesame oil combination.*

| | | |
|---|---|---|
| 2 cups | broken rice vermicelli | 500 mL |
| 8 oz | tofu | 250 g |
| 1/4 cup | soy sauce | 50 mL |
| 2 tbsp | sherry or Marsala wine | 25 mL |
| 1 | clove garlic, minced | 1 |
| 6 | green onions | 6 |
| 2 tbsp | butter | 25 mL |
| 1 tbsp | sesame oil | 15 mL |
| 1-1/2 cups | small broccoli florets | 375 mL |
| 1 cup | thinly sliced carrot | 250 mL |
| 10 | mushrooms, thickly sliced | 10 |
| 1 tbsp | slivered gingerroot | 15 mL |
| 2 tbsp | toasted sesame seeds | 25 mL |

● In large bowl, pour boiling water over vermicelli; let stand for 15 minutes. Drain well and set aside.

● Cut tofu into 3/4-inch (2 cm) thick slices; arrange in single layer in small dish. Combine soy sauce, sherry and garlic; pour over tofu and marinate for 10 minutes.

● Reserving 2 tbsp (25 mL) marinade, transfer slices to plate lined with double thickness of paper towels; cover with double thickness of paper towels. Place plate on top and weigh down with heavy cans; let stand for 3 minutes. Cut into 1/2-inch (1 cm) pieces. Set aside.

● Cut green onions diagonally into thin slices; set green and white parts aside separately.

● In skillet, heat butter with oil over medium heat; stir-fry white part of onions for 1 minute. Add broccoli and carrot; stir-fry for 4 minutes.

● Add mushrooms and ginger; stir-fry for 2 minutes. Add green part of onions and tofu; stir-fry for 2 minutes. Add vermicelli, reserved marinade and sesame seeds; toss gently and heat through. Makes 4 servings.

**TIP:** Pressing tofu before cooking with it helps keep it from crumbling. Look for firm or extra-firm tofu for this dish.

# Great Bakes

Under crispy golden toppings lie layers of deliciously melted cheese, tender pasta and a variety of vegetables, meats and seafood guaranteed to comfort and please.

## Easy Lasagna ▶

*Satisfying lasagna is a guaranteed crowd-pleaser at any potluck or buffet. Here's an easy-to-make version that delivers all the great taste with a minimum of work. Best of all, it can be made up to 1 day ahead.*

| | | |
|---|---|---|
| 8 oz | lasagna noodles | 250 g |
| 1 | pkg (10 oz/284 g) frozen chopped spinach, thawed and squeezed dry | 1 |
| 2 cups | shredded mozzarella cheese | 500 mL |
| 1/4 cup | freshly grated Parmesan cheese | 50 mL |
| | MEAT FILLING | |
| 8 oz | Italian sausage | 250 g |
| 8 oz | ground beef | 250 g |
| 1 | each onion, carrot and stalk celery, chopped | 1 |
| 4 | cloves garlic, minced | 4 |
| 1-1/2 tsp | each dried oregano and basil | 7 mL |
| Pinch | hot pepper flakes | Pinch |
| 1 | can (28 oz/796 mL) tomatoes | 1 |
| 1 | can (14 oz/398 mL) tomato sauce | 1 |
| 1/4 tsp | pepper | 1 mL |
| | CHEESE FILLING | |
| 2 | eggs | 2 |
| 1/4 tsp | each pepper and nutmeg | 1 mL |
| 2 cups | cottage cheese | 500 mL |
| 1 cup | shredded mozzarella cheese | 250 mL |
| 1/2 cup | freshly grated Parmesan cheese | 125 mL |

● MEAT FILLING: Remove sausage from casing; crumble meat. In Dutch oven, cook sausage and beef over medium-high heat, breaking up with spoon, for about 5 minutes or until no longer pink; remove to plate. Spoon off all but 1 tbsp (15 mL) fat from pot.

● Add onion, carrot, celery, garlic, oregano, basil and hot pepper flakes; cook, stirring, for 3 to 5 minutes or until softened. Add tomatoes, tomato sauce and meat; bring to boil. Reduce heat and simmer, breaking up tomatoes and stirring often, for 20 to 25 minutes or until thickened. Add pepper.

● CHEESE FILLING: In bowl, whisk together eggs, pepper and nutmeg. Blend in cottage cheese, mozzarella and Parmesan.

● Meanwhile, in large pot of boiling salted water, cook noodles for 6 to 8 minutes or until almost tender. Drain and cool in cold water. Remove and arrange in single layer on damp tea towel.

● Spread 1 cup (250 mL) of the meat filling as base in greased 13- x 9-inch (3 L) baking dish. Top with one-third of the noodles in single layer; spread with one-third of the remaining meat filling. Spread with half of the cheese filling, then half of the spinach. Starting with noodles, repeat layers once.

● Top with remaining noodles; spread with remaining meat filling. Sprinkle with mozzarella and Parmesan. Cover loosely with foil.

● Bake in 375°F (190°C) oven for 20 minutes. Uncover and bake for 20 to 25 minutes longer or until bubbling and heated through. Let stand for 10 minutes before serving. Makes 8 servings.

# Seafood and Spinach Lasagna

*Lobster and shrimp transform lasagna into special-occasion company fare. For good value, look to Atlantic frozen-pack shelled lobster — it's all meat. When mixed with shrimp and monkfish or sole, it feeds a group generously and stylishly.*

| | | |
|---|---|---:|
| 12 oz | spinach lasagna noodles | 375 g |
| | SEAFOOD LAYER | |
| 1 | onion, minced | 1 |
| 1 cup | dry white wine or fish stock | 250 mL |
| 1 lb | monkfish or sole | 500 g |
| 1 | can (11.3 oz/320 g) frozen lobster meat, thawed and drained | 1 |
| 8 oz | small cooked shrimp | 250 g |
| | SPINACH SAUCE | |
| 1/4 cup | butter | 50 mL |
| 1/4 cup | all-purpose flour | 50 mL |
| 3 cups | milk | 750 mL |
| 3 cups | shredded mozzarella cheese | 750 mL |
| 3/4 cup | freshly grated Parmesan cheese | 175 mL |
| 1 | pkg (10 oz/284 g) fresh spinach, cooked and squeezed dry | 1 |
| 1-1/2 tsp | salt | 7 mL |
| 1/2 tsp | each nutmeg and hot pepper sauce | 2 mL |

● SEAFOOD LAYER: In saucepan, bring onion and wine to simmer over low heat; cover and simmer for 5 minutes. Cut fish into 1/2-inch (1 cm) pieces; add to pan and simmer, covered, for 5 minutes. Pour into sieve set over large measure, reserving 1 cup (250 mL) liquid. Chop lobster into bite-size pieces; combine with fish mixture and shrimp.

● SPINACH SAUCE: In heavy saucepan, melt butter over medium heat; stir in flour and cook, whisking, for 2 minutes, without browning. Whisk in reserved fish-poaching liquid and milk; bring to boil. Reduce heat and simmer, whisking occasionally, for 5 minutes or until thickened and smooth; remove from heat. Stir in half of the mozzarella and Parmesan, the spinach, salt, nutmeg and hot pepper sauce.

● Meanwhile, in large pot of boiling salted water, cook noodles for 6 to 8 minutes or until almost tender. Drain and cool in cold water; remove and arrange in single layer on damp tea towel.

● Arrange 3 noodles in single layer in well-greased 13- x 9-inch (3 L) baking dish. Spread with one-quarter of the sauce and one-third of the seafood. Repeat layers twice. Top with remaining noodles, then sauce. Sprinkle with remaining mozzarella and Parmesan. *(Lasagna can be prepared to this point, covered and refrigerated for up to 8 hours. Add 10 minutes to baking time.)*

● Bake in 325°F (160°C) oven for 45 to 60 minutes or until golden brown and bubbling. Let stand for 10 minutes before serving. Makes 12 servings.

## COOKING SPINACH

● To cook fresh spinach, first rinse thoroughly in several changes of water, allowing sand to fall to bottom of sink. Slightly warm water relaxes crinkly leaves and releases more grit.

● Shake off excess water and transfer spinach to large heavy saucepan; cover and cook, with just the water clinging to leaves, over medium-high heat for about 5 minutes or until spinach has just wilted.

● Remove from heat and drain in sieve, pressing out moisture if spinach is destined for a stuffing or baked pasta layer.

● Frozen spinach can replace the fresh cooked spinach as a time-saver. Just let it thaw, press out excess moisture and follow instructions for cooked spinach.

# Lightened-Up Lasagna

| | | |
|---|---|---|
| 1 tbsp | olive oil | 15 mL |
| 1 | onion, chopped | 1 |
| 3 | green onions, chopped | 3 |
| 2 | cloves garlic, minced | 2 |
| 1/4 tsp | hot pepper flakes | 1 mL |
| 1 lb | ground chicken | 500 g |
| 1-1/2 cups | finely chopped sweet red pepper | 375 mL |
| 1 cup | each finely chopped carrots and celery | 250 mL |
| 2 | cans (each 28 oz/796 mL) tomatoes, puréed | 2 |
| 1 tsp | (approx) salt | 5 mL |
| 1/2 tsp | (approx) pepper | 2 mL |
| 1/4 cup | chopped fresh parsley | 50 mL |
| 2 cups | low-fat cottage cheese | 500 mL |
| 12 oz | lasagna noodles | 375 g |
| 2 cups | shredded low-fat mozzarella cheese (about 8 oz/250 g) | 500 mL |

● In Dutch oven, heat oil over medium heat; cook onion, green onions, garlic and hot pepper flakes for about 5 minutes or until softened. Add chicken; cook, stirring, for 5 minutes or until no longer pink.

● Add red pepper, carrots and celery; cook, stirring, for 5 minutes. Add tomatoes and bring to boil; add salt and pepper. Reduce heat to medium-low; simmer gently for 35 to 45 minutes or until thickened. Stir in parsley. Season cottage cheese with salt and pepper to taste.

● Meanwhile, in large pot of boiling salted water, cook noodles for 6 to 8 minutes or until almost tender. Drain and cool in cold water. Remove and arrange in single layer on damp tea towel.

● Arrange one-quarter of the noodles in single layer in greased 13- x 9-inch (3 L) baking dish. Spread with half of the cottage cheese and one-quarter of the sauce; sprinkle with one-quarter of the mozzarella. Repeat layer of noodles, sauce and mozzarella.

● Repeat layer of noodles, cottage cheese, sauce and mozzarella; top with layer of noodles, sauce and mozzarella. Cover with foil and bake in 375°F (190°C) oven for 50 minutes; uncover and bake for 10 minutes longer or until golden and bubbling. Let stand for 10 minutes before serving. Makes 8 servings.

*Reduced oil and low-fat ground chicken, cottage cheese and mozzarella make this lasagna lighter than most, and just as tasty.*

# Conchiglie with Zucchini and Spinach ◄

| | | |
|---|---|---|
| 1 | box (12 oz/375 g) jumbo conchiglie | 1 |
| 1 cup | freshly grated Parmesan cheese | 250 mL |
| | **FILLING** | |
| 3 | medium zucchini | 3 |
| | Salt | |
| 1 | bunch spinach (about 8 oz/250 g) | 1 |
| 1/4 cup | butter | 50 mL |
| 2 | onions, finely chopped | 2 |
| 1 | clove garlic, minced | 1 |
| 1 lb | ricotta cheese | 500 g |
| 1 cup | freshly grated Parmesan cheese | 250 mL |
| 2 | eggs | 2 |
| 1/4 cup | chopped fresh basil or parsley | 50 mL |
| 1/4 tsp | each pepper and nutmeg | 1 mL |
| | **SAUCE** | |
| 1/4 cup | butter | 50 mL |
| 2 | onions, finely chopped | 2 |
| 2 | cloves garlic, minced | 2 |
| 2 | cans (each 28 oz/796 mL) tomatoes | 2 |
| | Salt and pepper | |

● FILLING: Grate zucchini and place in colander. Sprinkle with 2 tsp (10 mL) salt; let drain for 30 minutes. Rinse and drain well; drain on paper towels.

● Trim spinach and rinse under water; shake off excess water. In saucepan, cover spinach and cook, with just the water clinging to leaves, over medium-high heat for about 5 minutes or just until wilted. Drain well and squeeze dry; chop coarsely and set aside.

● In large heavy skillet, melt butter over medium heat; cook onions and garlic for about 5 minutes or until tender. Add zucchini; cook until any moisture has evaporated. Add spinach and mix well. Let cool; drain off excess liquid.

● In large bowl, beat ricotta until smooth; beat in Parmesan, eggs, basil, 1 tsp (5 mL) salt, pepper and nutmeg. Stir in zucchini mixture until combined; set aside.

● SAUCE: In saucepan, melt butter over medium heat; cook onions and garlic for about 5 minutes or until softened. Add tomatoes, breaking up with spoon; cook for 30 to 45 minutes or until thickened. Purée in food processor; season with salt and pepper to taste. Set aside.

● In large pot of boiling salted water, cook conchiglie for 8 to 10 minutes or until tender but firm; drain and refresh under cold water. Gently shake conchiglie in colander to drain excess water. Coarsely chop any broken conchiglie; place in greased 13- x 9-inch (3 L) baking dish.

● Spoon some of the filling into each conchiglie; arrange, stuffed side up, over chopped ones. Pour sauce over top; sprinkle with Parmesan. Bake in 350°F (180° C) oven for 40 to 50 minutes or until bubbling. Makes 8 servings.

*Jumbo pasta shells (conchiglie), stuffed with a cheesy spinach and zucchini filling and napped with a robust tomato sauce, are more than worth the effort. This hearty vegetarian pasta dish is an excellent addition to any potluck supper.*

**TIP:** Jumbo pasta shells are easier to work with and fill than the tiny ones. If you can find only small shells, don't try to fill them. Simply layer them with the filling and sauce.

# Tuna Florentine ▾

*Spinach, which provides the Florentine touch, is a natural with pasta. Keep this easy dish in mind for weeknight suppers, and make it even easier by replacing the fresh spinach with a package of frozen.*

| | | |
|---|---|---|
| 2 tbsp | butter | 25 mL |
| 1 | onion, sliced | 1 |
| 1 | clove garlic, minced | 1 |
| 1 | can (19 oz/540 mL) tomatoes | 1 |
| 1 | can (7-1/2 oz/213 mL) tomato sauce | 1 |
| 1/2 tsp | each dried basil, granulated sugar and salt | 2 mL |
| 1/4 tsp | pepper | 1 mL |
| 4 oz | medium egg noodles | 125 g |
| 1 | pkg (10 oz/284 g) fresh spinach | 1 |
| 1 | can (6-1/2 oz/184 g) tuna, drained | 1 |
| 1/4 cup | freshly grated Parmesan cheese | 50 mL |

● In large skillet, melt butter over medium heat; cook onion and garlic for about 3 minutes or until softened. Stir in tomatoes, tomato sauce, basil, sugar, salt and pepper; simmer for about 20 minutes or until thickened.

● Meanwhile, in large pot of boiling salted water, cook noodles for 8 to 10 minutes or until tender but firm; drain well and set aside.

● Rinse spinach; shake off excess water. In saucepan, cover spinach and cook, with just the water clinging to leaves, over medium-high heat for about 5 minutes or just until wilted. Drain well and squeeze dry; chop coarsely and set aside.

● Break tuna into chunks and stir into tomato mixture along with cooked noodles. Transfer to 6-cup (1.5 L) casserole. Spoon chopped spinach around edge. Sprinkle Parmesan over top. Bake in 375°F (190°C) oven for about 25 minutes or until bubbling. Makes 4 to 6 servings.

# Nouvelle Tuna Casserole

| | | |
|---|---|---|
| 2 | pkg (each 10 oz/284 g) fresh spinach, trimmed | 2 |
| 1/3 cup | butter | 75 mL |
| 3 | onions, chopped | 3 |
| 1/2 cup | all-purpose flour | 125 mL |
| 6 cups | milk | 1.5 L |
| 2 tsp | each dried basil and salt | 10 mL |
| 1 tsp | pepper | 5 mL |
| Pinch | hot pepper flakes | Pinch |
| 4 cups | fusilli or penne | 1 L |
| 3 | cans (each 7-1/2 oz/213 g) tuna, drained and broken into chunks | 3 |
| 2 cups | shredded old Cheddar cheese | 500 mL |
| 2 tbsp | lemon juice | 25 mL |
| | TOPPING | |
| 3 cups | fresh bread crumbs | 750 mL |
| 1 cup | shredded old Cheddar cheese | 250 mL |
| 1 tbsp | butter, melted | 15 mL |
| 1 tbsp | Dijon mustard | 15 mL |

● Rinse spinach; shake off excess water. In stockpot, cover spinach and cook, with just the water clinging to leaves, over medium-high heat for about 5 minutes or just until wilted. Drain well and squeeze dry; chop coarsely and set aside.

● In large saucepan, melt butter over medium heat; cook onions for 3 minutes or until softened. Stir in flour; cook, whisking, for 3 minutes, without browning. Gradually whisk in milk until smooth; cook, whisking often, for about 15 minutes or until boiling and thickened. Reduce heat to low. Season with basil, salt, pepper and hot pepper flakes.

● Meanwhile, in large pot of boiling salted water, cook fusilli for 8 to 10 minutes or until tender but firm. Drain and refresh under cold water; drain again and return to pot. Add sauce, spinach, tuna, Cheddar and lemon juice; toss to combine. Divide between two greased 8-inch (2 L) square baking dishes, spreading evenly.

● TOPPING: Toss together bread crumbs, Cheddar, butter and mustard; sprinkle over casseroles. Cover loosely with foil. *(Casseroles can be prepared to this point, covered and refrigerated for up to 1 day or wrapped well and frozen for up to 2 months. Thaw completely in refrigerator. Bake for 25 to 30 minutes longer than specified, uncovering for last 10 minutes.)*

● Bake in 350°F (180°C) oven for 20 minutes; uncover and bake for 25 minutes longer or until heated through and golden. Makes 8 servings.

*Fresh spinach, old Cheddar, fusilli and basil update a family favorite. Since the recipe makes enough for two 8-inch (2 L) square baking dishes, enjoy one casserole right away and store the second in the freezer for up to 2 months.*

# Comfy Macaroni and Cheese

| | | |
|---|---|---|
| 2 cups | macaroni | 500 mL |
| 2 cups | shredded mozzarella cheese | 500 mL |
| 1-1/2 cups | sour cream | 375 mL |
| 1 cup | diced ham | 250 mL |
| 1 cup | cottage cheese | 250 mL |
| 1/2 cup | chopped sweet red pepper | 125 mL |
| 1 | egg, lightly beaten | 1 |
| 1/4 tsp | each salt and pepper | 1 mL |

● In large pot of boiling salted water, cook macaroni for 8 to 10 minutes or until tender but firm; drain well.

● In large bowl, combine 1-1/2 cups (375 mL) of the mozzarella, sour cream, ham, cottage cheese, red pepper, egg, salt and pepper. Add macaroni and mix well.

● Pour into greased 8-inch (2 L) square baking dish; sprinkle with remaining mozzarella. Bake in 350°F (180°C) oven for 30 minutes or until bubbling. Broil for 2 minutes or until lightly golden. Makes 4 servings.

*For most of us, macaroni was our introduction to pasta — cheese-rich and fork-tender under a crunchy topping. Here's an update with trendy peppers, a bit of ham and lots of creaminess from cottage cheese, mozzarella and sour cream.*

# Macaroni Tomato Pie

*This colorful variation on macaroni and cheese makes a quick and tasty supper any day of the week.*

| | | |
|---|---|---|
| 1-1/4 cups | macaroni | 300 mL |
| 1 | egg, beaten | 1 |
| 1-1/2 cups | shredded Cheddar cheese | 375 mL |
| 1 | can (19 oz/540 mL) stewed tomatoes | 1 |
| 1/4 tsp | each salt, pepper, dried oregano and basil | 1 mL |
| 1 cup | fresh bread crumbs | 250 mL |
| 1 tbsp | butter, melted | 15 mL |

● In large pot of boiling salted water, cook macaroni for 8 to 10 minutes or until tender but firm; drain well.

● Stir in egg and 1 cup (250 mL) of the Cheddar. Spread over bottom and side of greased 9-inch (23 cm) pie plate.

● Stir together tomatoes, salt, pepper, oregano and basil; pour into macaroni shell. Sprinkle with remaining Cheddar.

● Toss bread crumbs with butter; sprinkle over top, covering edge of macaroni shell. Bake in 350°F (180°C) oven for 25 to 30 minutes or until golden. Makes 4 servings.

# Cheesy Wild Mushroom Casserole

*It takes only a tiny package of wild mushrooms to boost the flavor of a whole panful of pasta. Choose dried porcini or morels, and add a bounty of fresh mushrooms.*

| | | |
|---|---|---|
| 7 cups | rigatoni | 1.75 L |
| 1 cup | shredded Fontina or Swiss cheese | 250 mL |
| 4 oz | Gorgonzola or mild blue cheese, crumbled | 125 g |
| 1-1/2 cups | freshly grated Parmesan cheese | 375 mL |
| | **MUSHROOM LAYER** | |
| 1-1/2 cups | warm water | 375 mL |
| 1 | pkg (1/2 oz/15 g) dried wild mushrooms | 1 |
| 1/4 cup | butter | 50 mL |
| 3 | onions, finely chopped | 3 |
| 6 cups | sliced fresh mushrooms (1 lb/500 g) | 1.5 L |
| 1/4 tsp | hot pepper flakes | 1 mL |
| | **SAUCE** | |
| 1/3 cup | butter | 75 mL |
| 1/2 cup | all-purpose flour | 125 mL |
| 4 cups | milk | 1 L |
| 1 tsp | salt | 5 mL |
| 1/4 tsp | pepper | 1 mL |

● In large pot of boiling salted water, cook rigatoni for 8 to 10 minutes or until tender but firm. Drain and refresh under cold water. Drain well; set aside.

● MUSHROOM LAYER: In bowl, pour warm water over dried mushrooms; soak for 30 minutes. Drain, straining liquid through cheesecloth-lined sieve; set liquid aside. Rinse mushrooms and chop; set aside.

● In large skillet, melt butter over medium heat; cook onions for about 5 minutes or until softened. Add fresh mushrooms, chopped wild mushrooms and hot pepper flakes; cook for 2 minutes. Add reserved soaking liquid; cook, stirring often, for 20 minutes or until no liquid remains. Remove from heat; set aside.

● SAUCE: In large saucepan, melt butter over medium heat; whisk in flour and cook, without browning, for 3 minutes. Whisk in milk; bring to boil, stirring constantly. Add salt and pepper; reduce heat and simmer, stirring often, for 5 to 7 minutes or until thickened.

● Arrange half of the rigatoni in greased 13- x 9-inch (3 L) baking dish. Spread with half of the mushroom mixture, then half of the sauce; scatter half each of the Fontina, Gorgonzola and Parmesan over top. Repeat layers.

● Bake in 350°F (180°C) oven for 40 to 50 minutes or until golden and bubbling. Makes 6 to 8 servings.

# Baked Chicken and Spinach Pasta ▼

| | | |
|---|---|---|
| 2 | pkg (each 10 oz/284 g) fresh spinach | 2 |
| 3-1/2 cups | penne | 875 mL |
| 1/3 cup | freshly grated Parmesan cheese | 75 mL |
| | **CHICKEN SAUCE** | |
| 2 tbsp | butter | 25 mL |
| 1/2 cup | diced ham | 125 mL |
| 2 | onions, chopped | 2 |
| 2 | cloves garlic, minced | 2 |
| 1 | carrot, diced | 1 |
| 1 | sweet red pepper, diced | 1 |
| 1-1/4 lb | ground chicken | 625 g |
| 1 | can (28 oz/796 mL) tomatoes, puréed | 1 |
| 2 tbsp | tomato paste | 25 mL |
| 1 tbsp | dried basil | 15 mL |
| 1 tsp | salt | 5 mL |
| 1/4 tsp | pepper | 1 mL |
| | **CHEESE SAUCE** | |
| 3 tbsp | butter | 45 mL |
| 1/4 cup | all-purpose flour | 50 mL |
| 3 cups | milk | 750 mL |
| 1-1/2 cups | shredded mozzarella cheese | 375 mL |
| 3/4 tsp | salt | 4 mL |
| 1/4 tsp | each pepper and nutmeg | 1 mL |

● CHICKEN SAUCE: In Dutch oven, melt butter over medium-high heat; cook ham, onions, garlic, carrot and red pepper for 10 minutes or until vegetables are softened. Using slotted spoon, transfer to dish; set aside.

● In same pan, cook chicken over high heat, breaking up with spoon, for 5 minutes or until no longer pink. Return ham mixture to pan along with tomatoes, tomato paste, basil, salt and pepper; bring to boil. Reduce heat and simmer for 30 minutes or until thickened.

● Meanwhile, rinse spinach; shake off excess water. In stockpot, cover spinach and cook, with just the water clinging to leaves, over medium-high heat for about 5 minutes or just until wilted. Drain well and squeeze dry; chop coarsely and set aside.

● CHEESE SAUCE: In heavy saucepan, melt butter over medium heat. Stir in flour; cook, stirring, for 2 minutes, without browning. Whisk in milk and bring to boil; reduce heat to medium-low and simmer, stirring often, for 5 minutes or until thickened. Stir in mozzarella, salt, pepper and nutmeg.

● Meanwhile, in large pot of boiling salted water, cook penne for 8 to 10 minutes or until tender but firm. Drain and toss with chicken sauce; spoon into 13- x 9-inch (3 L) baking dish, smoothing top. Top with spinach, then cheese sauce; sprinkle with Parmesan. Bake in 375°F (190°C) oven for about 45 minutes or until golden and bubbling. Let stand for 15 minutes. Makes 12 servings.

*T his up-to-date baked pasta is perfect for entertaining in the nineties — elegant yet effortless! Ground chicken in the sauce adds a taste surprise.*

# Asparagus Cannelloni ▶

*Even in the spring, a baked pasta is welcome, especially when it highlights the season's most popular vegetable — tender asparagus.*

| | | |
|---|---|---|
| 22 | precooked cannelloni tubes | 22 |
| 1/4 cup | freshly grated Parmesan cheese | 50 mL |
| | FILLING | |
| 1-1/2 lb | asparagus | 750 g |
| 1/3 cup | creamy goat cheese (chèvre) | 75 mL |
| 1 | egg | 1 |
| 1-1/2 cups | ricotta cheese | 375 mL |
| 1/3 cup | shredded mozzarella cheese | 75 mL |
| 1/2 tsp | grated lemon rind | 2 mL |
| 4 tsp | lemon juice | 20 mL |
| 3 | green onions, minced | 3 |
| 3/4 tsp | salt | 4 mL |
| Pinch | pepper | Pinch |
| | SAUCE | |
| 1/4 cup | butter | 50 mL |
| 1/4 cup | all-purpose flour | 50 mL |
| 3 cups | hot milk | 750 mL |
| 1/4 cup | shredded mozzarella cheese | 50 mL |
| 1/2 tsp | nutmeg | 2 mL |
| | Salt and pepper | |

● FILLING: Break off tough stems from asparagus; reserve for another use. Peel stems; cut into 1-inch (2.5 cm) lengths. In saucepan of boiling salted water, cook asparagus for about 10 minutes or until tender; drain. Transfer to food processor or blender; purée.

● In large bowl, beat goat cheese until smooth; gradually beat in egg and ricotta. Stir in asparagus, mozzarella, lemon rind and juice, onions, salt and pepper until well blended. Spoon into piping bag fitted with large plain tip; pipe into cannelloni tubes. Arrange in single layer in greased 13- x 9-inch (3 L) baking dish.

● SAUCE: In saucepan, melt butter over low heat; stir in flour and cook, whisking constantly, for 1 minute. Remove from heat and whisk in milk. Bring to boil over medium-high heat, stirring constantly. Reduce heat and simmer for 2 minutes. Add mozzarella, nutmeg, and salt and pepper to taste, stirring until cheese has melted.

● Pour sauce over cannelloni. Sprinkle with Parmesan. *(Recipe can be prepared to this point, covered and refrigerated for up to 2 days.)* Bake in 350°F (180°C) oven for 30 to 40 minutes or until bubbling. If desired, broil for 2 to 3 minutes or until lightly browned. Makes 8 servings.

## ASPARAGUS — A SURE SIGN OF SPRING!
*Celebrate the arrival of spring with tender, fresh asparagus.*

● Select firm, straight, rich-green spears that are uniform in size and have closed tips. Stalks should be well rounded: ridges are a sign of age. The thicker the spear, the tastier and more tender it is.

● Refrigerate for up to 3 days by wrapping the base of the stalks in damp paper towels and placing them in a plastic bag. Or, stand them in 1 inch (2.5 cm) of water and cover with plastic bag.

● Brush gently under cold running water to remove sand. Hold spear with both hands and snap off end; the stalk will break at the point where the toughness stops.

● Cook asparagus by layering spears in wide saucepan of boiling salted water and cooking for 2 to 5 minutes or until tender-crisp. Or, cook in steamer basket over boiling water for the same time.

# Macaroni and Cheese Oven Omelette

*Thursday night and the crisper looks bare. Ditto the meat tray. Thank goodness for some pasta, eggs, cheese and a frozen vegetable in the freezer. Peas can replace the spinach, if desired; you'll need 1 cup (250 mL).*

| | | |
|---|---|---|
| 1 cup | macaroni | 250 mL |
| 1 | pkg (10 oz/300 g) frozen spinach, thawed | 1 |
| 1 tbsp | vegetable oil | 15 mL |
| 1 | onion, chopped | 1 |
| 3/4 tsp | salt | 4 mL |
| 1/2 tsp | pepper | 2 mL |
| 8 | eggs, beaten | 8 |
| 1-1/2 cups | shredded old Cheddar cheese | 375 mL |
| 1/4 cup | dry bread crumbs | 50 mL |
| 1/4 tsp | dried sage | 1 mL |

● In large pot of boiling salted water, cook macaroni for 8 to 10 minutes or until tender but firm; drain, reserving 1/2 cup (125 mL) cooking water.

● Meanwhile, in sieve, press out moisture from spinach; chop spinach and set aside. In 8-inch (20 cm) ovenproof skillet, heat oil over medium heat; cook onion, stirring, for 5 minutes or until softened. Remove from heat; stir in macaroni, spinach, salt and pepper.

● Combine eggs with 1 cup (250 mL) of the Cheddar and reserved cooking water; pour evenly over macaroni mixture. Sprinkle with remaining Cheddar, bread crumbs and sage.

● Bake in 350°F (180°C) oven for about 25 minutes or until puffed and knife inserted in center comes out clean. Makes 4 servings.

# Cheese and Sausage Cannelloni

*There are three things that have streamlined this robust pasta dish. First, fresh lasagna rectangles rolled around the filling replace fiddly-to-fill cannelloni tubes. The freshness of this pasta also eliminates the boiling step, and since the sausage and spaghetti sauce are already seasoned, fewer ingredients are needed to create a full-flavored dish.*

| | | |
|---|---|---|
| 2 tbsp | olive oil | 25 mL |
| 1 | small onion, finely chopped | 1 |
| 1 | clove garlic, minced | 1 |
| 1 | each carrot and stalk celery, diced | 1 |
| 3/4 tsp | dried basil | 4 mL |
| 1/4 tsp | salt | 1 mL |
| Pinch | pepper | Pinch |
| 1 lb | Italian sausage | 500 g |
| 1/3 cup | red wine | 75 mL |
| 2 tbsp | tomato paste | 25 mL |
| 3/4 cup | ricotta cheese | 175 mL |
| 1 | egg | 1 |
| 1 | pkg (10 oz/300 g) frozen chopped spinach, thawed and squeezed dry | 1 |
| 12 | fresh lasagna rectangles (6- x 5-inches/15 x 12 cm) | 12 |
| 1-1/2 cups | shredded mozzarella cheese | 375 mL |
| 4 cups | Fast and Easy Spaghetti Sauce (recipe, p. 70) | 1 L |
| 1/4 cup | freshly grated Parmesan cheese | 50 mL |

● In large skillet, heat oil over medium heat; cook onion, garlic, carrot and celery for about 5 minutes or until softened. Stir in basil, salt and pepper; cook, stirring, for 1 minute.

● Remove sausage from casings. Add to skillet; cook, breaking up into small pieces, for about 10 minutes or until no longer pink. Drain off fat. Stir in wine and tomato paste until combined. Remove from heat; let cool slightly. Stir in ricotta, egg and spinach.

● Arrange lasagna in single layer on work surface. Spoon 1/3 cup (75 mL) filling along one long edge of each rectangle. Sprinkle 1 cup (250 mL) of the mozzarella evenly over filling. Starting at long edge, roll up each into cylinder.

● Pour 1-1/2 cups (375 mL) of the spaghetti sauce into 13- x 9-inch (3 L) baking dish, spreading evenly. Nestle stuffed cylinders snugly on top. Pour remaining tomato sauce over top; sprinkle with Parmesan and remaining mozzarella.

● Cover loosely with foil; bake in 350°F (180°C) oven for 20 minutes; uncover and bake for 10 minutes longer or until golden and bubbling. Makes 6 servings.

# Baked Vegetable Spaghetti

| | | |
|---|---|---|
| 2 tbsp | olive oil | 25 mL |
| 2 | large onions, chopped | 2 |
| 3 | cloves garlic, minced | 3 |
| 4 | zucchini, diced | 4 |
| 1 | each sweet green and yellow pepper, diced | 1 |
| 1 | eggplant, peeled and diced | 1 |
| 2 | cans (each 19 oz/540 mL) tomatoes | 2 |
| 1 | can (5-1/2 oz/156 mL) tomato paste | 1 |
| 2 tsp | dried basil | 10 mL |
| 1 tsp | each dried oregano, granulated sugar and salt | 5 mL |
| 1/2 tsp | pepper | 2 mL |
| 1/4 tsp | dried thyme | 1 mL |
| 1 lb | spaghetti | 500 g |
| 1/4 cup | freshly grated Parmesan cheese | 50 mL |
| | CHEESE SAUCE | |
| 1/4 cup | butter | 50 mL |
| 1/4 cup | all-purpose flour | 50 mL |
| 2 cups | milk | 500 mL |
| 1 cup | shredded mozzarella cheese | 250 mL |
| 1/2 tsp | salt | 2 mL |
| 1/4 tsp | pepper | 1 mL |

● In Dutch oven, heat half of the oil over medium-high heat; cook onions, garlic, zucchini, sweet peppers and eggplant, stirring often, for 5 to 10 minutes or until starting to soften.

● Add tomatoes, tomato paste, basil, oregano, sugar, salt, pepper and thyme; bring to boil. Reduce heat and simmer for 25 to 30 minutes or until slightly thickened.

● CHEESE SAUCE: In saucepan, melt butter over medium heat; stir in flour and cook, whisking, for 2 minutes, without browning. Gradually whisk in milk and bring to boil; reduce heat to medium-low and cook, whisking, for about 10 minutes or until thickened. Stir in mozzarella, salt and pepper until melted.

● Meanwhile, in large pot of boiling salted water, cook spaghetti for 5 minutes or until almost tender but still firm. Drain and toss with remaining olive oil and vegetable mixture.

● Transfer spaghetti mixture to 13- x 9-inch (3 L) baking dish, spreading evenly. Spoon cheese sauce over top. Sprinkle with Parmesan. *(Spaghetti can be cooled, covered and refrigerated for up to 1 day or frozen for up to 2 weeks. Thaw in refrigerator for 48 hours. Add 10 minutes to baking time.)*

● Bake on baking sheet in 350°F (180°C) oven for about 1 hour or until golden and heated through. Makes 8 servings.

W*hen serving a crowd, it's always a good idea to provide a vegetarian dish such as this three-layer casserole — spaghetti, summery ratatouille and mozzarella topping — for guests who don't eat meat.*

## FREEZING CASSEROLES

To freeze, let casserole cool thoroughly in refrigerator. Overwrap with plastic wrap and enclose in airtight plastic container or large freezer bag. To thaw, remove from container and place in refrigerator. Because casseroles are often dense, they take 1 to 2 days to thaw completely.

# Pastitsio Pie ▶

*Creamy custard-topped pastitsio is as soothing and satisfying as lasagna, with an added touch of the exotic — wisps of cinnamon in the beef sauce and nutmeg in the cheese custard.*

| | | |
|---|---|---|
| 1 tbsp | butter | 15 mL |
| 1 | onion, chopped | 1 |
| 3 | cloves garlic, minced | 3 |
| 1-1/2 lb | lean ground beef | 750 g |
| 1/2 tsp | each dried oregano, cinnamon and salt | 2 mL |
| 1/4 tsp | pepper | 1 mL |
| 1 | can (14 oz/398 mL) stewed tomatoes | 1 |
| 1 | can (5-1/2 oz/156 mL) tomato paste | 1 |
| 1 tbsp | red wine vinegar | 15 mL |
| 1/4 cup | chopped fresh parsley | 50 mL |
| 2 cups | macaroni | 500 mL |
| 2 tbsp | dry bread crumbs | 25 mL |
| 1 cup | freshly grated Parmesan cheese | 250 mL |
| | SAUCE | |
| 2 tbsp | butter | 25 mL |
| 2 tbsp | all-purpose flour | 25 mL |
| 1 cup | milk | 250 mL |
| 1 cup | cottage cheese | 250 mL |
| 1 | egg | 1 |
| Pinch | each nutmeg, salt and pepper | Pinch |

● In nonstick skillet, melt half of the butter over medium heat; cook onion and garlic, stirring, for 3 minutes. Stir in beef, oregano, cinnamon, salt and pepper; cook, stirring, for 7 to 10 minutes or until no longer pink. Drain off fat. Stir in tomatoes, tomato paste and vinegar; cook, stirring, for 3 minutes. Remove from heat; stir in parsley. Set aside.

● Meanwhile, in large pot of boiling salted water, cook macaroni for 8 to 10 minutes or until tender but firm. Drain and refresh under cold water; drain again and set aside.

● SAUCE: In saucepan, melt butter over medium heat; stir in flour and cook, whisking, for 2 minutes, without browning. Gradually whisk in milk and cook, whisking, for about 5 minutes or until thickened; remove from heat. Stir in cottage cheese, egg, nutmeg, salt and pepper.

● Grease 10-inch (25 cm) deep pie plate with remaining butter; sprinkle with bread crumbs. Spoon in half of the macaroni. Spread meat mixture evenly over top, pressing down lightly; sprinkle with one-third of the Parmesan.

● Spoon remaining macaroni over top; carefully pour sauce over macaroni. *(Pie can be covered and refrigerated for up to 1 day. Let stand at room temperature for 30 minutes; add 10 minutes to baking time.)*

● Sprinkle with remaining Parmesan. Bake on baking sheet in 350°F (180°C) oven for 50 to 60 minutes or until golden. Makes 6 servings.

# Long Simmers

Time, and only time, can work its magic on flavors — mellowing here, concentrating there — to create sauces with exquisite depth and robust elegance.

## Abruzzi-Style Spaghetti

*Glen Antonacci, originator of this deliciously thick and smooth spaghetti sauce, uses tomato paste and juice instead of tomatoes — in the style of his home region of Abruzzi, Italy.*

| | | |
|---|---|---|
| 1-1/2 lb | pork spareribs | 750 g |
| 1 lb | Calabrian sausage with fennel seeds and paprika | 500 g |
| 3/4 cup | (approx) freshly grated Parmesan cheese | 175 mL |
| 1/2 cup | Italian-seasoned bread crumbs | 125 mL |
| 2 tbsp | dried basil | 25 mL |
| 4 | cloves garlic, minced | 4 |
| 1 tbsp | granulated sugar | 15 mL |
| 1/2 tsp | pepper | 2 mL |
| 1 | can (48 oz/1.36 L) tomato juice | 1 |
| 1 | can (5-1/2 oz/156 mL) tomato paste | 1 |
| 1-1/2 lb | spaghetti | 750 g |
| | Chopped fresh parsley | |

● Cut spareribs into 2- or 3-rib portions. Cut sausage into 3-inch (8 cm) lengths. Set aside.

● In large heavy saucepan or Dutch oven, combine cheese, bread crumbs, basil, garlic, sugar and pepper. Add tomato juice and paste, whisking to blend in paste.

● Add spareribs and sausage; bring to boil over medium heat. Reduce heat to very low and simmer, stirring occasionally, for about 2 hours or until thickened and meat is tender enough to fall off bones.

● Meanwhile, in large pot of boiling salted water, cook spaghetti for 8 to 10 minutes or until tender but firm; drain well.

● Remove sausage and spareribs; arrange around edge of warmed serving platter. Toss spaghetti with about 2 cups (500 mL) of the sauce; arrange in center of meat. Sprinkle with parsley and more cheese. Serve remaining sauce in pitcher alongside platter. Makes 6 to 8 servings.

**TIP:** Ingredients such as prosciutto (Italian ham) and pancetta (Italian bacon) are more widely available now that many Italian products have gone supermarket-mainstream. However, mild ham and lean bacon can replace them both, and any good fresh (not smoked or dried) Italian sausage can replace the Calabrian sausage.

---

### STORING MEAT SAUCES
The first step to storing a meaty sauce is to chill it quickly. If there is a large quantity, transfer it to a large shallow airtight container and refrigerate it, uncovered, until completely cold. Cover and freeze, or use within a day or two or according to time recommended in recipe.

# Tomato and Wild Mushroom Linguine

| | | |
|---|---|---|
| 1 | pkg (1/2 oz/15 g) dried wild mushrooms | 1 |
| 1 tbsp | olive oil | 15 mL |
| 1 | small onion, chopped | 1 |
| 2 | cloves garlic, minced | 2 |
| 4 | slices prosciutto, chopped | 4 |
| 3 cups | sliced fresh mushrooms (12 oz/375 g) | 750 mL |
| 1 | can (28 oz/796 mL) tomatoes, chopped | 1 |
| 1 tsp | salt | 5 mL |
| 3/4 tsp | each pepper and dried thyme | 4 mL |
| 8 oz | linguine | 250 g |
| | Freshly grated Parmesan cheese | |

● Rinse dried mushrooms under cold water. Soak for 15 minutes in 1 cup (250 mL) boiling water. Strain through cheesecloth-lined sieve, reserving liquid. Rinse mushrooms and chop coarsely; set aside.

● In saucepan, heat oil over medium heat; cook onion, garlic and prosciutto, stirring, for 3 minutes or until onion is softened. Add fresh mushrooms and reserved soaking liquid; cook, stirring gently, for 10 to 15 minutes or until liquid is reduced to half.

● Stir in tomatoes, soaked mushrooms, salt, pepper and thyme; bring to boil. Reduce heat and simmer, stirring occasionally, for about 25 minutes or until thickened.

● Meanwhile, in large pot of boiling salted water, cook linguine for 8 to 10 minutes or until tender but firm; drain well. Toss with sauce; sprinkle with Parmesan to taste. Makes 2 servings.

A *few dried porcini or morel mushrooms give a rich, woodsy taste to a pasta sauce. But if fresh mushrooms are all you have, by all means use fresh, adding another cup (250 mL) to the quantity in the recipe.*

# Spaghetti Bolognese

| | | |
|---|---|---|
| 3 tbsp | vegetable oil | 50 mL |
| 1 | onion, chopped | 1 |
| 2 | cloves garlic, minced | 2 |
| 1 | each carrot and stalk celery, finely diced | 1 |
| 1 lb | ground beef | 500 g |
| 1 cup | white wine | 250 mL |
| 1/2 cup | milk | 125 mL |
| 1-1/4 tsp | salt | 6 mL |
| 3/4 tsp | pepper | 4 mL |
| Pinch | nutmeg | Pinch |
| 1 | can (28 oz/796 mL) tomatoes, chopped | 1 |
| 2 tbsp | tomato paste | 25 mL |
| 1 | bay leaf | 1 |
| 12 oz | spaghetti | 375 g |
| | Freshly grated Parmesan cheese | |
| | Chopped fresh parsley | |

● In large heavy saucepan, heat oil over medium-low heat; cook onion, garlic, carrot and celery, stirring, for about 5 minutes or until softened.

● Add beef; cook, stirring to break up, for about 10 minutes or just until no longer pink, being careful not to brown. Drain off fat.

● Pour in wine; increase heat to medium-high and cook, stirring occasionally, until wine has evaporated. Add milk, salt, pepper and nutmeg; cook, stirring, until milk has evaporated.

● Add tomatoes, tomato paste and bay leaf; bring to boil. Reduce heat to low and cook, stirring occasionally, for about 2 hours or until thickened. Discard bay leaf.

● Meanwhile, in large pot of boiling salted water, cook spaghetti for 8 to 10 minutes or until tender but firm; drain well.

● In warmed serving bowl, toss spaghetti with half of the sauce. Top with remaining sauce. Sprinkle with Parmesan and parsley to taste. Makes 4 servings.

T*his is ragu, the mother of all spaghetti sauces — and worth every minute it takes to simmer the beef with tomatoes, bay leaf and the surprise ingredient, milk. While unexpected here, milk is traditionally added in Italy because it keeps the meat deliciously tender through the long and slow simmering.*

# Italian Sausage and Tomato Fettuccine

*The long simmer brings out the sweetness of the onion and carrot, tempering the acidity of the tomatoes. While the red wine is optional, it is recommended for the balance it brings to the sausage and vegetables.*

| | | |
|---|---|---|
| 3 tbsp | olive oil | 50 mL |
| 1 | onion, chopped | 1 |
| 2 | cloves garlic, minced | 2 |
| 1 | each large carrot and stalk celery, finely diced | 1 |
| 1 cup | sliced mushrooms (4 oz/125 g) | 250 mL |
| 1 | sweet green pepper, chopped | 1 |
| 2 tbsp | (approx) chopped fresh parsley | 25 mL |
| 2 tsp | dried basil | 10 mL |
| 1 tsp | salt | 5 mL |
| 3/4 tsp | pepper | 4 mL |
| 1 lb | Italian sausage with fennel seeds | 500 g |
| 1 | can (28 oz/796 mL) tomatoes, chopped | 1 |
| 1/2 cup | red wine (optional) | 125 mL |
| 1/4 cup | tomato paste | 50 mL |
| 12 oz | fettuccine or fusilli | 375 g |
| | Freshly grated Parmesan cheese | |

● In Dutch oven or large saucepan, heat oil over medium heat; cook onion, garlic, carrot, celery, mushrooms, green pepper, parsley, basil, salt and pepper for 3 to 5 minutes or until softened.

● Remove sausage from casings. Add to saucepan; cook, breaking up into small pieces, for 5 minutes or until no longer pink. Stir in tomatoes, wine (if using) and tomato paste; bring to boil. Reduce heat and simmer, stirring occasionally, for 1-1/2 hours or until thickened.

● Meanwhile, in large pot of boiling salted water, cook fettuccine for 8 to 10 minutes or until tender but firm; drain well.

● In warmed serving bowl, toss fettuccine with half of the sauce. Pour remaining sauce over top; sprinkle with Parmesan and more parsley to taste. Makes 4 servings.

**TIP:** If sausage with fennel seeds is unavailable in your area, use regular Italian sausage and add 1 tbsp (15 mL) crushed fennel seeds to the tomato sauce.

## PAIRING PASTA WITH SAUCES

*It's important to make a good match between pasta shapes and sauces. Where possible in our recipes, we have suggested several complementary pasta choices for a sauce. At the same time, we've left room for personal taste and preference, so do feel free to enjoy your favorite sauce with the pasta you like best!*

● **Long, thin pastas** such as fettuccine and spaghetti work well with tomato, cream, and butter and cheese sauces; strong-flavored sauces with garlic or anchovies; and fish or seafood sauces.

● Team up **short, curled or twisted pasta** shapes such as fusilli, penne and conchiglie with meat or vegetable sauces because the pasta traps tasty morsels inside and you can pick up both the pasta and chunks of meat or vegetables at the same time.

● **Small pastas** such as macaroni are good in a minestrone or a soup with legumes.

● **Flat, short pastas** such as farfalle are best coated in a delicate cream, cheese or vegetable sauce.

# Fusilli with Meatball Stew ▼

| | | |
|---|---|---|
| 1 | large onion, chopped | 1 |
| 4 | cloves garlic, minced | 4 |
| 2-1/4 cups | halved mushrooms (8 oz/250 g) | 550 mL |
| 2 tsp | dried basil | 10 mL |
| 3/4 tsp | dried sage | 4 mL |
| 1/4 tsp | hot pepper flakes | 1 mL |
| 4 tsp | all-purpose flour | 20 mL |
| 1-1/2 cups | beef stock | 375 mL |
| 3 tbsp | tomato paste | 50 mL |
| 1 tbsp | red wine vinegar | 15 mL |
| 1 | bay leaf | 1 |
| 3 | carrots, sliced | 3 |
| 1/2 tsp | (approx) salt | 2 mL |
| 1 | each sweet red and yellow pepper, chopped | 1 |
| 1 | zucchini, halved and sliced | 1 |
| 1 cup | frozen peas | 250 mL |
| | Pepper | |
| 1 lb | fusilli lunghi | 500 g |
| | | |
| | MEATBALLS | |
| 1-1/2 lb | lean ground beef | 750 g |
| 1 | small onion, minced | 1 |
| 1 | egg | 1 |
| 2 tbsp | freshly grated Parmesan cheese | 25 mL |
| 1 tsp | dried basil | 5 mL |
| 1/2 tsp | salt | 2 mL |
| 1/4 tsp | each dried sage and pepper | 1 mL |
| 4 tsp | vegetable oil | 20 mL |

● MEATBALLS: In bowl, combine beef, onion, egg, Parmesan, basil, salt, sage and pepper; shape into 18 meatballs. In Dutch oven, heat oil over medium-high heat; cook meatballs, turning often, for 8 to 12 minutes or until well browned. Drain on paper towel.

● Drain off all but 1 tbsp (15 mL) fat from pan; cook onion, garlic, mushrooms, basil, sage and hot pepper flakes, stirring, for about 3 minutes or until onion is softened.

● Sprinkle with flour; cook, stirring, for 1 minute. Gradually pour in stock, scraping up brown bits; bring to boil.

● Stir in tomato paste, vinegar, bay leaf, carrots and salt; add meatballs. Reduce heat to low and simmer, partially covered, for 20 to 30 minutes or until carrots are almost tender. Stir in red and yellow peppers; cook for 1 minute. *(Stew can be prepared to this point and refrigerated in airtight container for up to 1 day or frozen for up to 2 months; thaw and reheat over medium heat.)*

● Add zucchini and peas; simmer for 5 to 10 minutes or until tender. Discard bay leaf. Season with more salt and pepper to taste.

● Meanwhile, in large pot of boiling salted water, cook fusilli for 8 to 10 minutes or until tender but firm; drain well. Arrange on plates; top with stew. Makes 6 servings.

*Warm up a cold evening with a simmered meatball-and-vegetable stew to serve over curly long fusilli. Pass freshly grated Parmesan to sprinkle on each serving.*

# Spaghetti with Meatballs

*The Fast and Easy Spaghetti Sauce (this page) is the starting point for this saucy meatball recipe. You can also use 4 cups (1 L) of any good-quality purchased spaghetti sauce when time is short.*

| | | |
|---|---|---|
| 3/4 lb | ground beef | 375 g |
| 1 | egg | 1 |
| 1/4 cup | dry bread crumbs | 50 mL |
| 1/2 tsp | salt | 2 mL |
| 1/2 tsp | each dry mustard and basil | 2 mL |
| 1/4 tsp | pepper | 1 mL |
| | Fast and Easy Spaghetti Sauce (recipe, this page) | |
| 12 oz | spaghetti | 375 g |
| 1/4 cup | freshly grated Parmesan cheese | 50 mL |
| 2 tbsp | chopped fresh basil or parsley | 25 mL |

● In large bowl, mix together beef, egg, bread crumbs, salt, mustard, basil and pepper. Form into 1-inch (2.5 cm) meatballs; place on rimmed baking sheet.

● Bake in 400°F (200°C) oven for 15 to 20 minutes or until no longer pink inside. Drain off fat.

● In large saucepan, heat spaghetti sauce until simmering. Add meatballs and simmer for 10 minutes.

● Meanwhile, in large pot of boiling salted water, cook spaghetti for 8 to 10 minutes or until tender but firm; drain well and toss with Parmesan. Arrange on warmed serving platter; spoon sauce over top. Sprinkle with fresh basil. Makes 4 servings.

# Fast and Easy Spaghetti Sauce

*What to cook when the cupboard is almost bare? If there's some spaghetti and a big can of tomatoes, this to-the-rescue recipe offers a quick and delicious weeknight supper.*

| | | |
|---|---|---|
| 2 tbsp | olive oil | 25 mL |
| 1 | onion, chopped | 1 |
| 3 | cloves garlic, minced | 3 |
| 1 | each carrot and stalk celery, diced | 1 |
| 1-1/2 cups | sliced mushrooms (6 oz/175 g) | 375 mL |
| 1 | sweet green pepper, chopped | 1 |
| 1 tsp | dried basil | 5 mL |
| 3/4 tsp | salt | 4 mL |
| Pinch | hot pepper flakes (optional) | Pinch |
| 1 | can (28 oz/796 mL) tomatoes, puréed | 1 |
| 1/4 cup | tomato paste | 50 mL |

● In large saucepan, heat oil over medium-high heat; cook onion, garlic, carrot, celery, mushrooms and green pepper for 8 to 10 minutes or until softened.

● Stir in basil, salt, and hot pepper flakes (if using); cook, stirring, for 1 minute. Pour in tomatoes and tomato paste; bring to boil. Reduce heat and simmer for about 30 minutes or until thickened. Makes 4 cups (1 L).

### THE BEST TOMATOES FOR SAUCE

When making a fresh tomato sauce, the best tomatoes to choose are plum tomatoes. These pear-shaped tomatoes are meatier and drier than round slicing tomatoes and make a thicker, tastier sauce in less time. Take a tip from Italian families who preserve tomatoes every summer — spread out garden-picked or store-bought plum tomatoes in a single layer to ripen fully to an intense red.

# Winter's Big-Batch Tomato Sauce

| | | |
|---|---|---|
| 2 tbsp | olive oil | 25 mL |
| 2 tbsp | chopped onions | 25 mL |
| 4 | cloves garlic, minced | 4 |
| 1 tsp | granulated sugar | 5 mL |
| 1 tsp | each dried basil, oregano and salt | 5 mL |
| 1/2 tsp | each dried thyme and pepper | 2 mL |
| 4 | carrots, diced | 4 |
| 2 | stalks celery, chopped | 2 |
| 1 | sweet green pepper, chopped | 1 |
| 3 | cans (each 28 oz/796 mL) stewed tomatoes | 3 |
| 1 cup | tomato paste | 250 mL |

● In large heavy saucepan, heat oil over medium heat; cook onions and garlic for 3 minutes or until softened.

● Stir in sugar, basil, oregano, salt, thyme and pepper. Add carrots, celery and green pepper; cook, stirring, for 3 minutes.

● Stir in tomatoes and tomato paste; bring to boil. Reduce heat and simmer, stirring occasionally, for 45 to 60 minutes or until thickened slightly. Makes 12 cups (3 L).

*Even in winter, you can simmer a fine pasta sauce from scratch. This one makes enough to see you through three or four meals — a toss with pasta, a lasagna, a pizza or even a sauce for chicken or fish.*

# Summer's Fresh Herb Tomato Sauce

| | | |
|---|---|---|
| 1/3 cup | olive oil | 75 mL |
| 3 | stalks celery, chopped | 3 |
| 2 | large carrots, chopped | 2 |
| 1 | onion, chopped | 1 |
| 1 | large clove garlic, minced | 1 |
| 9 lb | plum tomatoes (about 4 dozen) | 4 kg |
| 2 tsp | each chopped fresh basil and oregano | 10 mL |
| 1 tsp | granulated sugar | 5 mL |
| 1/2 tsp | salt | 2 mL |
| 1/4 tsp | pepper | 1 mL |
| 1/4 tsp | fennel seeds | 1 mL |
| 1 | bay leaf | 1 |

● In large heavy saucepan or Dutch oven, heat oil over medium heat; cook celery, carrots, onion and garlic, stirring often, for 15 minutes or until tender but not browned.

● Trim, core and coarsely chop tomatoes; add to pan and bring to simmer. Cook, mashing occasionally, for 45 to 60 minutes or until vegetables are tender. Pass through medium disk of food mill or through conical ricer; pour into large clean saucepan.

● Add basil, oregano, sugar, salt, pepper, fennel seeds and bay leaf; bring to simmer. Cook, stirring frequently, for 1-1/2 to 2 hours or until thickened. Discard bay leaf.

● Pour sauce into airtight containers, leaving 1/2-inch (1 cm) headspace; freeze. Makes about 12 cups (3 L).

*Summertime — and the garden is overflowing. Why not freeze a taste of the harvest to enjoy all winter long? For convenience, freeze this summer-fresh sauce in quantities that suit your household's favorite recipes.*

# Putting up Tomatoes ▶

*Nothing can beat the convenience and taste of home-canned tomatoes — ready to simmer into a sauce, or toss into a soup or stew. Here's how to capture the summer harvest in a cannerful of tomatoes that will last all winter long.*

| 18 lb | firm ripe tomatoes (about 8 dozen plum or 4 dozen round) | 8 kg |
| --- | --- | --- |
| | Citric acid or reconstituted lemon juice | |

● Wash and rinse canning jars and bands. About 45 minutes before filling jars, fill boiling water bath canner two-thirds full of water; heat to just below boil and keep hot.

● Place jars in rack set on edge of canner or in 225°F (110°C) oven to heat. A few minutes before filling jars, bring pot of water to boil; boil lids for 5 minutes. Remove from heat; leave in water until ready to use.

● In large pot of boiling water, blanch tomatoes, in batches, for 30 to 60 seconds or until skins loosen. Remove and chill in cold water; drain immediately and peel. Core and trim away any green, bruised or decayed spots; cut into quarters.

● In two large pots or in batches, over high heat, heat tomatoes until heated through and juices boil, about 10 minutes.

● Filling one jar at a time, pack tomatoes and juice into jar, leaving 1/2-inch (*or* 2 cm) headspace. For each 4-cup (1 L) jar, add 1/2 tsp (2 mL) citric acid *or* 2 tbsp (25 mL) reconstituted lemon juice. (For each

2 cup/500 mL jar, add 1/4 tsp/1 mL citric acid *or* 1 tbsp/15 mL reconstituted lemon juice.)

● Run spatula around inside of jar, pressing tomatoes to release any air bubbles. Add more tomatoes or juice if needed to maintain 1/2-inch (*or* 2 cm) headspace.

● With clean damp cloth, wipe rim. Cover with lid; screw on band firmly without forcing (fingertip tight). Place on rack set on edge of canner. Lower filled rack into water.

● Pour in enough simmering water, avoiding tops of jars, to cover jars by 1 to 2 inches (2.5 to 5 cm). Cover canner and bring to full rolling boil. Boil 4-cup (1 L) jars for 45 minutes, 2-cup (500 mL) jars for 35 minutes. Turn off heat.

● Lift rack to sit on edge of canner. Using jar lifter, transfer jars to towel-lined surface. Let cool completely (some separation of juice in jars is natural). Do not retighten screw bands.

● Check for seal to ensure lids curve inward and don't move when pressed with finger. Refrigerate any improperly sealed jars; use within 3 days. Store in cool, dark, dry place. Store in refrigerator after opening. Makes about 28 cups (7 L).

## FOR BEST RESULTS

● Letting tomatoes ripen fully before canning (see sidebar, p. 70) makes for a richer-colored and tastier home-canned product. Plum tomatoes are best since they are less watery than the beefsteak variety and cook up into a thicker, more flavorful sauce. Be sure to can only firm ripe tomatoes, not overripe, soft ones.

● It is safe to can tomatoes in a boiling water canner; other vegetables require pressure canning. Don't add vegetables when canning tomatoes; add them when preparing a dish.

● Always use new lids. Reuse bands if not bent or rusty. Use canning jars that are free of nicks and cracks.

# Magnifico Salads

Main dish, side dish, make-ahead or last-minute toss —
pasta salads are sensational any way you serve them. Here's
our pick of the classics plus the hottest new tastes.

## Antipasto Fusilli Salad

*This simple salad has lots of old-fashioned Italian flavor. It also travels well, making it ideal for picnics or for the cottage. Tricolor pasta adds color.*

| | | |
|---|---|---|
| 3 cups | fusilli | 750 mL |
| 1/2 cup | extra virgin olive oil | 125 mL |
| 1/4 cup | white wine vinegar | 50 mL |
| 2 tbsp | water | 25 mL |
| 1/2 tsp | each dried oregano, basil and dry mustard | 2 mL |
| 1/4 tsp | each dried rosemary and black pepper | 1 mL |
| 1 | clove garlic, minced | 1 |
| 1 | can (19 oz/540 mL) chick-peas or kidney beans, drained and rinsed | 1 |
| 1 | each carrot and zucchini, finely diced | 1 |
| 1/2 cup | freshly grated Parmesan cheese | 125 mL |
| | Salt | |

| | | |
|---|---|---|
| | Lettuce leaves | |
| 1 cup | cherry tomatoes | 250 mL |

● In large pot of boiling salted water, cook fusilli for 8 to 10 minutes or until tender but firm; drain well.

● Meanwhile, in large bowl, whisk together oil, vinegar, water, oregano, basil, mustard, rosemary, pepper and garlic. Stir in warm pasta to coat thoroughly.

● Add chick-peas, carrot, zucchini, Parmesan, and salt to taste. *(Salad can be refrigerated for up to 1 day.)* Spoon onto lettuce-lined plates; top with tomatoes. Makes 6 servings.

## Greek Pasta Salad

*Bow-tie pasta (farfalle) is an excellent choice for salads — it's firm enough to withstand cooking, tossing and a day in the refrigerator without getting mushy.*

| | | |
|---|---|---|
| 8 cups | farfalle | 2 L |
| 1/2 cup | extra virgin olive oil | 125 mL |
| 1/3 cup | lemon juice | 75 mL |
| 1 tbsp | anchovy paste | 15 mL |
| 2 | cloves garlic, minced | 2 |
| 1 tsp | dried oregano | 5 mL |
| Pinch | each salt and pepper | Pinch |
| 1 | small cucumber | 1 |
| 2 cups | small cherry tomatoes | 500 mL |
| 1 cup | small black olives | 250 mL |
| 1 cup | chopped red onion | 250 mL |
| 1/2 cup | chopped fresh parsley | 125 mL |
| 1 cup | finely diced feta cheese (about 4 oz/125 g) | 250 mL |

● In large pot of boiling salted water, cook farfalle for 8 to 10 minutes or until tender but firm; drain well.

● Meanwhile, whisk together oil, lemon juice, anchovy paste, garlic, oregano, salt and pepper; toss half with pasta. Let cool to room temperature, stirring occasionally.

● Cut cucumber in half lengthwise. Scoop out seeds and thinly slice crosswise. Add to pasta along with tomatoes, olives, onion, parsley and remaining dressing; toss to coat well. Gently stir in feta cheese. *(Salad can be covered and refrigerated for up to 1 day.)* Makes about 10 servings.

# Choose-Your-Fish Pasta Salad ▲

| | | |
|---|---|---|
| 3 cups | rotini | 750 mL |
| 1 | can (19 oz/540 mL) red kidney beans, drained and rinsed | 1 |
| 4 | green onions, chopped | 4 |
| 2 | sweet green peppers, chopped | 2 |
| 1/2 cup | sliced black olives | 125 mL |
| 2 | cans (each 7-1/2 oz/213 g) salmon or tuna (or 2 cups/500 mL flaked grilled or cooked fish) | 2 |
| 2 | tomatoes, chopped | 2 |
| 1 | head leaf lettuce or 2 bunches watercress | 1 |
| | **DRESSING** | |
| 1/3 cup | red wine vinegar | 75 mL |
| 1/4 cup | lemon juice | 50 mL |
| 3 | large cloves garlic, minced | 3 |
| 1 tbsp | dried oregano | 15 mL |
| 1 tsp | salt | 5 mL |
| 1/2 tsp | pepper | 2 mL |
| 1/2 cup | extra virgin olive oil | 125 mL |

● In large pot of boiling salted water, cook rotini for 8 to 10 minutes or until tender but firm. Drain and refresh under cold water; drain well.

● DRESSING: Meanwhile, in small bowl, combine vinegar, lemon juice, garlic, oregano, salt and pepper; gradually whisk in oil.

● In large bowl, combine pasta, beans, green onions, green peppers and olives; toss lightly with half of the dressing. *(Salad can be prepared to this point, covered and refrigerated for up to 1 day.)*

● Drain salmon and break up into chunks; add to bowl along with tomatoes and remaining dressing. Toss lightly. Line plates with lettuce; top with salad. Makes 6 servings.

*I*t's your pick — tuna, salmon or leftover cooked fish — in this colorful red bean and rotini salad.

# Ham and Artichoke Heart Salad

*Summer — and with a big bowl of pasta salad, meal-making certainly is easy. If you want to pack this salad for a picnic, don't chop and mix in the tomato until you're ready to eat.*

| | | |
|---|---|---|
| 2-1/2 cups | penne | 625 mL |
| 2 cups | chopped green beans | 500 mL |
| 1 | large tomato | 1 |
| 1 | sweet red pepper | 1 |
| 6 | green onions | 6 |
| 1 | jar (6 oz/170 mL) marinated artichoke hearts | 1 |
| 8 oz | cooked ham, cut into strips | 250 g |
| | Pepper | |
| 2 tbsp | chopped fresh parsley | 25 mL |
| | **DRESSING** | |
| 1/4 cup | cider vinegar | 50 mL |
| 1 tbsp | grainy mustard | 15 mL |
| 2 tsp | Dijon mustard | 10 mL |
| 1 | clove garlic, minced | 1 |
| 1/2 tsp | salt | 2 mL |
| 1/2 cup | extra virgin olive oil | 125 mL |

● In large pot of boiling salted water, cook penne for 7 minutes. Add green beans; cook for 3 minutes or until tender-crisp and pasta is tender but firm. Drain and refresh under cold water; drain well and place in large bowl.

● Meanwhile, coarsely chop tomato. Seed and cut red pepper in half crosswise; cut into thin strips. Slice green onions. Drain artichoke hearts, reserving 1 tbsp (15 mL) marinade; cut hearts in half.

● Add tomato, red pepper, green onions, artichoke hearts and ham to pasta mixture.

● DRESSING: In small bowl, whisk together vinegar, grainy and Dijon mustards, garlic and salt; gradually whisk in oil. Whisk in reserved artichoke marinade. Pour over salad; toss gently to combine. Season with pepper to taste. Garnish with parsley. Makes 4 to 6 servings.

# Garden Pasta Salad

*Dressings for pasta salads need lots of flavor, and two kinds of mustard (grainy and Dijon) provide it here. Sturdy short pasta such as rotelle (cartwheel shapes) is the best choice for salads.*

| | | |
|---|---|---|
| 2 | carrots, sliced | 2 |
| 1 | sweet red pepper, thinly sliced | 1 |
| Half | red onion, coarsely chopped | Half |
| 1 | head broccoli | 1 |
| 1 | zucchini | 1 |
| 2-1/2 cups | rotelle | 625 mL |
| | **DRESSING** | |
| 1 cup | plain yogurt | 250 mL |
| 2 tbsp | Dijon mustard | 25 mL |
| 1 tbsp | grainy mustard | 15 mL |
| 1 | clove garlic, minced | 1 |
| 1/4 tsp | each salt and pepper | 1 mL |
| Pinch | granulated sugar | Pinch |
| 2 tbsp | chopped fresh basil or parsley | 25 mL |

● Place carrots, red pepper and onion in large salad bowl.

● Cut broccoli into bite-size florets; reserve stalks for another use. Cut zucchini in half lengthwise; slice crosswise.

● In large pot of boiling salted water, cook rotelle for 7 minutes. Add broccoli; cook for 2 minutes. Add zucchini; cook for 1 minute. Drain and refresh under cold water; drain well and add to vegetables in bowl.

● DRESSING: Stir together yogurt, Dijon and grainy mustards, garlic, salt, pepper and sugar; pour over vegetables and toss gently. Sprinkle with basil. Makes 4 to 6 servings.

**TIP:** This refreshing salad is also wonderful with a variety of add-ins — 1 can of drained tuna, 2 cups (500 mL) leftover cooked flaked salmon, 2 cups (500 mL) julienned ham or 1-1/2 cups (375 mL) cubed cheese.

# Grilled Vegetable and Fusilli Salad

| 1 | each sweet red, green and yellow pepper | 1 |
|---|---|---|
| 2 | zucchini | 2 |
| 12 oz | mushrooms | 375 g |
| 1 | red onion | 1 |
| 1/4 cup | vegetable oil | 50 mL |
| 2-1/3 cups | fusilli | 575 mL |
| | DRESSING | |
| 1/3 cup | chopped fresh basil | 75 mL |
| 1/4 cup | red wine vinegar | 50 mL |
| 1 tbsp | Dijon mustard | 15 mL |
| 2 | cloves garlic, minced | 2 |
| 3/4 tsp | each salt and pepper | 4 mL |
| 1/2 cup | extra virgin olive oil | 125 mL |

● Place red, green and yellow peppers on greased grill over medium-high heat; cook, turning often, for 20 to 25 minutes or until charred. Let cool slightly; peel, seed and cut into thick strips. Place in large bowl.

● Meanwhile, cut zucchini diagonally into 1/2-inch (1 cm) thick slices. Trim stems from mushrooms. Cut onion into 8 wedges. Lightly brush vegetables with oil.

● Place mushrooms and onion on grill; cook, turning occasionally, for 8 to 10 minutes or until tender. Remove and set aside. Place zucchini on grill; cook for 10 to 15 minutes or until tender. Cut mushrooms, onions and zucchini into quarters. Add to sweet peppers in bowl.

● DRESSING: In small bowl, whisk together basil, vinegar, mustard, garlic, salt and pepper; gradually whisk in oil. Pour over vegetables; marinate for at least 8 hours or up to 24 hours.

● In large pot of boiling salted water, cook fusilli for 8 to 10 minutes or until tender but firm. Drain and refresh under cold water; drain well and toss with vegetable mixture. Makes 4 servings.

*Grilled peppers, zucchini and mushrooms add a new twist to pasta salad. Garnish with fresh basil leaves and cherry tomatoes.*

# Pasta Salad Niçoise

| 3 cups | penne or fusilli | 750 mL |
|---|---|---|
| 2 | tomatoes, coarsely chopped | 2 |
| 1 | sweet green or yellow pepper, cut into strips | 1 |
| Half | red onion, sliced | Half |
| 1 | can (7 oz/198 g) tuna, drained and broken into chunks | 1 |
| 1/2 cup | sliced black olives | 125 mL |
| 2 tbsp | chopped fresh basil | 25 mL |
| | Pepper | |
| 2 | hard-cooked eggs | 2 |
| | DRESSING | |
| 3 tbsp | red wine vinegar | 50 mL |
| 1 tbsp | lemon juice | 15 mL |
| 1 tsp | Dijon mustard | 5 mL |
| 1/2 tsp | salt | 2 mL |
| 1 | clove garlic, minced | 1 |
| 1/3 cup | extra virgin olive oil | 75 mL |

● In large pot of boiling salted water, cook penne for 8 to 10 minutes or until tender but firm. Drain and refresh under cold water; drain well and place in salad bowl. Add tomatoes, green pepper, onion, tuna and olives.

● DRESSING: In small bowl, whisk together vinegar, lemon juice, mustard, salt and garlic; gradually whisk in oil. Pour over pasta mixture; add basil and toss gently to combine. Season with pepper to taste. Quarter eggs; arrange over salad. Makes 4 servings.

*A Niçoise salad usually includes potatoes, but this pasta variation is a delicious change.*

# Curried Chicken Pasta Salad

*Chicken salad is like a story that gets told over and over again because everyone likes it — and each time, it's a little different. Here, it's exotic with a curry-yogurt dressing and radiatore (radiator-shaped) pasta.*

| | | |
|---|---|---|
| 1 tbsp | vegetable oil | 15 mL |
| 1 tsp | curry powder | 5 mL |
| 1 tsp | liquid honey | 5 mL |
| 4 | boneless skinless chicken breasts | 4 |
| 2-1/2 cups | radiatore | 625 mL |
| 1 | large sweet green pepper, chopped | 1 |
| 3 | carrots, sliced | 3 |
| 4 | green onions, sliced | 4 |
| 1/3 cup | currants | 75 mL |
| 1/2 cup | chopped toasted almonds (see p. 25) | 125 mL |
| | DRESSING | |
| 3/4 cup | plain yogurt | 175 mL |
| 3/4 cup | buttermilk | 175 mL |
| 1 tsp | curry powder | 5 mL |
| 1 tsp | liquid honey | 5 mL |
| 1/4 tsp | each dry mustard and ground coriander | 1 mL |
| 1/4 tsp | each salt and pepper | 1 mL |
| Pinch | cinnamon | Pinch |
| 3 tbsp | chopped fresh coriander | 50 mL |

● In small bowl, stir together oil, curry powder and honey; brush over one side of chicken breasts. Place on greased grill over medium-high heat; cook, turning once and brushing other side with remaining honey mixture, for 12 to 14 minutes or until no longer pink inside. Let cool slightly; cut into bite-size strips.

● Meanwhile, in large pot of boiling salted water, cook radiatore for 8 to 10 minutes or until tender but firm. Drain and refresh under cold water; drain well.

● In large salad bowl, combine radiatore, green pepper, carrots, green onions, currants and chicken.

● DRESSING: In separate bowl, stir together yogurt, buttermilk, curry powder, honey, mustard, ground coriander, salt, pepper and cinnamon. Stir in 2 tbsp (25 mL) of the chopped coriander. Pour over salad; toss gently to combine. Garnish with remaining coriander and almonds. Makes 4 to 6 servings.

# Chicken and Tomato Pasta Salad

*Leftover grilled chicken is sensational in a pasta salad, especially with summer-fresh basil and tomatoes.*

| | | |
|---|---|---|
| 4 cups | penne | 1 L |
| 2 cups | trimmed snow peas | 500 mL |
| 2 | large tomatoes | 2 |
| 1/3 cup | light mayonnaise | 75 mL |
| 1/4 cup | buttermilk | 50 mL |
| 1 | clove garlic, minced | 1 |
| 1/4 tsp | each salt and pepper | 1 mL |
| 2 | cooked chicken breasts, cut into chunks | 2 |
| 1/3 cup | chopped fresh basil | 75 mL |
| | Fresh basil leaves | |

● In large pot of boiling salted water, cook penne for 8 to 10 minutes or until tender but firm. Add snow peas; cook for 1 minute. Drain and refresh under cold water; drain well.

● Meanwhile, core tomatoes. Chop one tomato coarsely and set aside. Quarter remaining tomato; purée in food processor or blender. Add mayonnaise, buttermilk, garlic, salt and pepper; purée until smooth.

● In large bowl, toss together dressing, pasta mixture, reserved tomato, chicken and chopped basil. Garnish with basil leaves. Makes 4 servings.

# Grilled Chicken and Noodle Salad ▼

| | | |
|---|---|---|
| 2 cups | trimmed snow peas | 500 mL |
| 4 | boneless skinless chicken breasts | 4 |
| 1 tbsp | vegetable oil | 15 mL |
| 8 oz | buckwheat noodles* | 250 g |
| 2 cups | bean sprouts | 500 mL |
| 1/2 cup | unsalted roasted peanuts, chopped | 125 mL |
| 1/2 cup | slivered Spanish onion | 125 mL |
| 1/4 cup | snipped chives or green onions (green part only) | 50 mL |
| | Tamari* | |
| | **DRESSING** | |
| 2/3 cup | light mayonnaise | 150 mL |
| 1/4 cup | water | 50 mL |
| 3 tbsp | tahini* | 45 mL |
| 3 tbsp | tamari | 45 mL |
| 4 tsp | sesame oil | 20 mL |
| Dash | hot pepper sauce | Dash |

● DRESSING: Whisk together mayonnaise, water, tahini, tamari, sesame oil and hot pepper sauce. *(Dressing can be covered and refrigerated for up to 1 day.)*

● In pot of boiling water, cook snow peas for 1 minute or until tender-crisp. Drain and refresh under cold water; pat dry. *(Snow peas can be wrapped in tea towel and refrigerated for up to 8 hours.)*

● Brush chicken with oil; cook on greased grill over medium-high heat, turning once, for 12 to 15 minutes or until no longer pink inside. Let cool slightly; slice thinly on diagonal.

● Meanwhile, in large pot of boiling salted water, cook noodles for 5 minutes or until tender but firm. Drain and refresh under cold water; drain again. *(Noodles can be set aside in bowl of cold water in refrigerator for up to 2 hours; drain.)*

● In bowl, toss together dressing, noodles, bean sprouts, peanuts, onion, chives and snow peas. In middle of each salad plate, drizzle about 1 tsp (5 mL) tamari; mound noodle mixture on top. Fan chicken around noodle mixture. Makes 4 servings.

*\* Buckwheat noodles (soba), tahini (sesame paste) and tamari (soy sauce) are available at some specialty and health food stores.*

*If you can't find buckwheat noodles (soba), you can use whole wheat spaghetti with delicious results.*

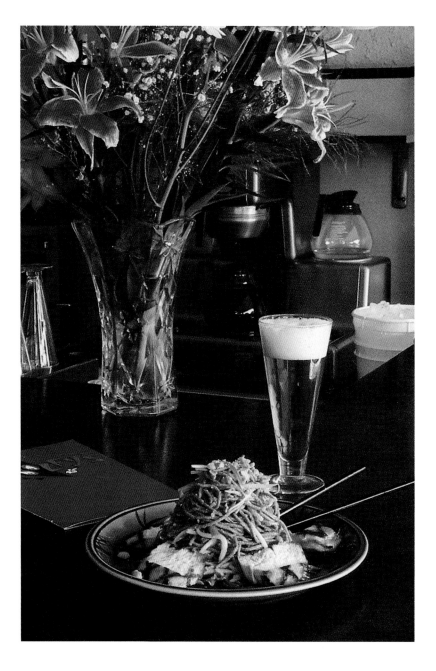

# Old-Fashioned Macaroni Salad

*Here's old-fashioned flavor with some new-fashioned, lower-fat ingredients such as light mayonnaise and low-fat yogurt or sour cream.*

| | | |
|---|---|---|
| 2-1/2 cups | macaroni | 625 mL |
| 2 | each carrots and stalks celery, finely diced | 2 |
| 1 | sweet red pepper, finely diced | 1 |
| 4 | green onions, finely chopped | 4 |
| 1 cup | shredded mozzarella cheese | 250 mL |
| 1/2 cup | finely chopped dill pickles | 125 mL |
| 1/4 cup | chopped fresh parsley | 50 mL |
| | DRESSING | |
| 1 cup | light mayonnaise | 250 mL |
| 3/4 cup | plain yogurt or low-fat sour cream | 175 mL |
| 2 tbsp | Dijon mustard | 25 mL |
| 1 tbsp | lemon juice | 15 mL |
| 1/4 tsp | each salt and pepper | 1 mL |

● In large pot of boiling salted water, cook macaroni for 8 to 10 minutes or until tender but firm. Drain and refresh under cold water until thoroughly chilled; drain well.

● In large bowl, combine macaroni, carrots, celery, red pepper, green onions, mozzarella and pickles.

● DRESSING: Stir together mayonnaise, yogurt, mustard, lemon juice, salt and pepper. Pour over macaroni mixture; toss gently until thoroughly combined. Garnish with parsley. Makes 4 servings.

# Winter Vegetable Pasta Toss

*Preparation of the pasta and winter vegetables for this hearty warm salad is simplified by cooking them together in one pot.*

| | | |
|---|---|---|
| 8 oz | butternut squash | 375 g |
| 1-1/2 cups | julienned peeled rutabaga or carrots | 375 mL |
| 2-3/4 cups | farfalle | 675 mL |
| 5 | green onions, chopped | 5 |
| 1/4 cup | chopped fresh parsley | 50 mL |
| | Salt and pepper | |
| | VINAIGRETTE | |
| 1/4 cup | apple juice | 50 mL |
| 3 tbsp | canola oil | 45 mL |
| 2 tbsp | cider vinegar | 25 mL |
| 1 tbsp | Dijon mustard | 15 mL |
| Pinch | each salt and pepper | Pinch |

● VINAIGRETTE: In small bowl, whisk together apple juice, oil, vinegar, mustard, salt and pepper; set aside.

● Peel and cut squash into 1- x 1/2-inch (2.5 x 1 cm) pieces; set aside.

● In large pot of boiling salted water, cook rutabaga and farfalle for 5 minutes. Add squash; cook for 6 to 7 minutes or just until vegetables are tender and pasta is tender but firm. Drain well.

● Toss pasta mixture with vinaigrette, green onions and parsley. Season with salt and pepper to taste. Makes 4 servings.

**TIP:** To julienne rutabaga or carrots, cut into sticks about 2 inches (5 cm) long and the thickness of a pencil.

# Pack-and-Go Rotini Salad ▲

| 1/2 cup | extra virgin olive oil | 125 mL |
|---------|------------------------|--------|
| 4 | cloves garlic, minced | 4 |
| 8 cups | rotini | 2 L |
| 1/2 cup | finely chopped fresh basil | 125 mL |
| 1 | sweet yellow pepper, diced | 1 |
| 1 cup | mild or medium salsa | 250 mL |
| 1 tbsp | red wine vinegar | 15 mL |
|  | Salt and pepper |  |
| 4 | firm ripe tomatoes | 4 |

● In small saucepan, combine 1/4 cup (50 mL) of the oil with garlic; heat over low heat for 5 minutes or until fragrant.

● Meanwhile, in large pot of boiling salted water, cook rotini for 8 to 10 minutes or until tender but firm; drain well.

● In large bowl, toss pasta with garlic mixture and remaining oil. Add basil, yellow pepper, salsa and vinegar; toss well. Season with salt and pepper to taste. Let cool completely. *(Salad can be prepared to this point, covered and refrigerated for up to 1 day.)*

● Halve and seed tomatoes; cut into large cubes. Toss with salad just before serving. Makes 12 servings.

*This is a great salad to make for a reunion picnic or big barbecue buffet. Just add the tomatoes at serving time.*

# Broccoli and Rotini Salad ▲

*This main-course salad is equally good warm or at room temperature.*

| | | |
|---|---|---:|
| 2 | bunches broccoli (2 lb/1 kg) | 2 |
| 6 cups | rotini or penne | 1.5 L |
| 1/4 cup | raisins | 50 mL |
| 1/2 cup | extra virgin olive oil | 125 mL |
| 4 | cloves garlic, minced | 4 |
| 1/4 tsp | hot pepper flakes | 1 mL |
| 3 | anchovy fillets, minced | 3 |
| 1/3 cup | toasted pine nuts | 75 mL |
| 2 tbsp | chopped fresh basil | 25 mL |
| 1 tbsp | lemon juice | 15 mL |
| | Salt and pepper | |

● Cut broccoli into 2-inch (5 cm) pieces. In large pot of boiling salted water, cook broccoli for 5 to 8 minutes or until tender.

Remove with slotted spoon and refresh under cold water; drain, pat dry and transfer to large serving bowl.

● Add rotini to water in pot; cook for 8 to 10 minutes or until tender but firm. Drain and refresh under cold water; drain well. Add to broccoli.

● Meanwhile, in small bowl, cover raisins with boiling water. Let stand for 20 minutes; drain.

● In skillet, heat oil over low heat; cook garlic, hot pepper flakes and anchovies, stirring, for 3 to 4 minutes or until garlic is tender. Let cool slightly; add to pasta mixture. Add raisins, pine nuts, basil, lemon juice, and salt and pepper to taste; toss to combine. Makes 6 servings.

# Buckwheat Noodle Salad

| | | |
|---|---|---|
| 6 | dried shiitake mushrooms | 6 |
| 1 tbsp | tamari (see p.79) or soy sauce | 15 mL |
| 8 oz | buckwheat noodles or whole wheat spaghetti | 250 g |
| 1 tbsp | sesame oil | 15 mL |
| 1 | English cucumber, diced | 1 |
| 1/2 cup | chopped walnuts | 125 mL |
| 3 tbsp | chopped fresh coriander or parsley | 50 mL |
| 1 | head leaf lettuce, separated | 1 |
| 1/2 cup | sliced radishes | 125 mL |
| | DRESSING | |
| 2 tbsp | tahini (see p. 79) or crunchy peanut butter | 25 mL |
| 2 tbsp | tamari or soy sauce | 25 mL |
| 1/4 cup | cider vinegar | 50 mL |
| 2 tbsp | sesame oil | 25 mL |
| 1 tbsp | minced gingerroot | 15 mL |
| 1/2 tsp | hot pepper flakes | 2 mL |
| 1/4 tsp | pepper | 1 mL |
| 1 | clove garlic, minced | 1 |

● DRESSING: In small bowl, whisk together tahini and tamari until smooth. Whisk in vinegar, oil, ginger, hot pepper flakes, pepper and garlic; set aside.

● In separate small bowl, cover mushrooms with boiling water; stir in tamari. Let stand for 15 minutes. Drain and rinse well; discard stems. Slice caps into slivers.

● Meanwhile, in large pot of boiling salted water, cook noodles for 5 minutes or until tender but firm. Drain and refresh under cold water; drain well.

● In bowl, toss noodles with oil. Add mushrooms, cucumber, walnuts, coriander and dressing; toss well.

● Line salad bowl or platter with lettuce; top with noodle mixture. Garnish with radishes. Makes 6 servings.

*East meets West in an appetizing blend of exotic and fresh flavors. This vegetarian main-course salad is a fine buffet dish.*

# Pesto Spaghetti Salad

| | | |
|---|---|---|
| 1 lb | spaghetti or fusilli lunghi | 500 g |
| 5 | carrots, sliced | 5 |
| 2 cups | cauliflower florets | 500 mL |
| 2 | sweet red, yellow or green peppers, cut into chunks | 2 |
| 1 cup | Presto Pesto (recipe, p. 19) | 250 mL |

● In large pot of boiling salted water, cook spaghetti for 5 minutes. Add carrots, cauliflower and red pepper; cook for 5 minutes or until tender-crisp and spaghetti is tender but firm. Drain and refresh under cold water; drain well and place in bowl.

● Add Presto Pesto and toss to combine. *(Salad can be refrigerated for up to 8 hours.)* Makes 4 servings.

*Green and cool for a summer supper, this salad can be made with whatever summer vegetables you fancy. Serve sliced cold meat or devilled eggs alongside.*

# Thai Vegetable Noodles

| 10 | snow peas | 10 |
|---|---|---|
| 12 oz | spaghetti | 375 g |
| 1 | sweet red pepper, diced | 1 |
| 1/2 cup | sliced water chestnuts, julienned | 125 mL |
| 1/3 cup | shredded fresh basil | 75 mL |
| 1/4 cup | chopped green onion | 50 mL |
| Half | can (14 oz/398 mL) baby corn cobs, drained | Half |
| 2 tbsp | toasted sesame seeds (see TIP, this page) | 25 mL |
| | DRESSING | |
| 1/3 cup | rice vinegar or white wine vinegar | 75 mL |
| 1/3 cup | hoisin sauce | 75 mL |
| 3 tbsp | each vegetable and sesame oil | 45 mL |
| 3 tbsp | soy sauce | 45 mL |
| 1 tbsp | minced gingerroot | 15 mL |
| 1-1/2 tsp | dry mustard | 7 mL |
| 1-1/2 tsp | granulated sugar | 7 mL |
| 2 | cloves garlic, minced | 2 |

● DRESSING: In bowl, whisk together vinegar, hoisin sauce, vegetable and sesame oils, soy sauce, ginger, mustard, sugar and garlic; set aside.

● In large pot of boiling water, blanch snow peas for 1 minute. Remove with slotted spoon and refresh under cold water; pat dry. Set aside.

● Add spaghetti to boiling water; cook for 8 to 10 minutes or until tender but firm. Drain well.

● In large bowl, toss together warm spaghetti, red pepper, water chestnuts, basil, onion, snow peas and two-thirds of the dressing; let cool slightly, about 5 minutes.

● Add remaining dressing; toss to mix. Garnish with baby corn cobs and sesame seeds. Makes 6 servings.

*Spaghetti goes Oriental with water chestnuts and a zesty rice vinegar dressing. This moist salad is best served warm.*

# Spicy Sesame Noodles ◄

| 1-1/4 lb | fresh Chinese wheat noodles | 625 g |
|---|---|---|
| 1/4 cup | toasted sesame seeds (see TIP, this page) | 50 mL |
| 1/3 cup | chicken stock | 75 mL |
| 1/4 cup | soy sauce | 50 mL |
| 3 tbsp | rice vinegar | 45 mL |
| 4 tsp | hoisin sauce | 20 mL |
| 1 tbsp | chili oil (or 1/2 tsp/2 mL hot pepper sauce) | 15 mL |
| 2 tsp | sesame oil | 10 mL |
| 1/2 tsp | granulated sugar | 2 mL |
| 1/4 tsp | pepper | 1 mL |
| Half | each cucumber and cantaloupe | Half |
| 6 | green onions, chopped | 6 |
| 1/2 cup | chopped fresh coriander | 125 mL |
| 1/3 cup | chopped toasted walnuts | 75 mL |

● In large pot of boiling salted water, cook noodles for 5 to 7 minutes or until tender but firm. Drain and refresh under cold water; drain well and set aside.

● In bowl, combine sesame seeds, stock, soy sauce, rice vinegar, hoisin sauce, chili oil, sesame oil, sugar and pepper; add noodles and toss. Arrange on platter.

● Peel, seed and julienne cucumber and cantaloupe. Sprinkle over noodle mixture along with onions, coriander and walnuts. Makes 8 servings.

**TIP:** To toast sesame seeds, cook in small skillet over medium heat, stirring, for 3 to 6 minutes or until golden.

*Melon and cucumber add freshness to a tangy, chili-spiked tangle of noodles. Toast walnuts in a skillet after the sesame seeds.*

# Making Fresh Pasta

*Making your own pasta takes a little time, but you'll find the delicious fresh taste is worth every crank of the pasta machine. If you don't have a pasta machine, get out your rolling pin and follow our hand-rolled method. All of these pastas are scrumptious tossed with grated cheese, fresh herbs and butter — or see PRESTO PASTAS for tasty inspirations.*

## HAND-ROLLED FRESH PASTA

You can make your own fresh pasta even if you don't have a pasta machine.

● Prepare dough as outlined in steps 1 and 2 below.

● Follow step 3 and let dough rest for 1 hour before rolling out each piece with rolling pin to 1/16-inch (1.5 mm) thickness, rotating dough often and lightly dusting with flour to prevent sticking.

● Follow step 6.

● Roll up dough jelly roll-style into flat roll about 4 inches (10 cm) wide. Using sharp knife, cut roll crosswise into 1/4-inch (5 mm) wide strips. Unroll strips.

| 2 cups | all-purpose flour | 500 mL |
|---|---|---|
| 3 | eggs | 3 |
| 1/4 tsp | salt | 1 mL |

### VARIATIONS

SPINACH PASTA: Cook 4 cups (1 L) trimmed fresh spinach until wilted. Drain, let cool and squeeze dry; chop finely to make about 1/3 cup (75 mL). Reduce eggs to 2. Add spinach to eggs and salt; mix well before incorporating flour.

SAFFRON PASTA: Add 1/8 tsp (0.5 mL) ground saffron to eggs and salt; mix well before incorporating flour.

ROASTED RED PEPPER PASTA: Broil 1 sweet red pepper, turning several times, for about 20 minutes or until blistered and charred. Let cool; peel, seed and chop finely. In food processor or blender, purée to make about 1/3 cup (75 mL). Reduce eggs to 2. Add purée to eggs and salt; mix well before incorporating flour.

FRESH BASIL PASTA: Add 1/4 cup (50 mL) chopped fresh basil to eggs and salt; mix well before incorporating flour.

**1** Mound flour on work surface; make well in center. Add eggs and salt to well.

**2** Using fork, beat eggs with salt. Starting from inside edge and working around well, gradually incorporate flour into egg mixture until soft dough is formed. Scoop up and sift any flour left on work surface, discarding any bits of dough; set aside.

**3** On clean lightly floured surface, knead dough for 10 minutes, working in enough of the sifted flour to make dough smooth and elastic. Cover with plastic wrap and let rest for 20 minutes. Divide dough into 3 pieces to make handling easier; cover.

**4** On lightly floured surface, roll out one of the dough pieces into 5-inch (12 cm) long strip; dust with flour. Feed through widest setting of pasta machine rollers 4 times or until edges form smooth line, folding dough in half and lightly flouring after each pass through machine.

**5** Set machine to next narrowest setting; run pasta through once without folding. Repeat running dough through rollers until next-to-finest setting is reached, cutting dough in half if awkwardly long. Lightly flour dough; run through finest setting. Repeat with remaining dough.

**6** Using pasta rack or broomstick balanced between two chairs, hang dough for 15 to 20 minutes or until leathery but not dry. (If dough dries, remove from rack and pat with damp cloth.)

**7** Change setting from rolling to cutting position. Cut pasta into lengths of up to 10 inches (25 cm). Feed each length through cutter. *(Pasta can be covered with plastic wrap and kept at room temperature for up to 1 hour, stored in refrigerator for up to 2 days or frozen for up to 2 months.)* Makes 12 oz (375 g).

# The Contributors

## Test Kitchen

## Photography Credits

FRED BIRD:
    9, 12, 15, 16, 19, 20,
    24, 31, 33, 34, 37, 38,
    41, 43, 47, 49, 51, 54,
    56, 59, 65, 69, 73, 75,
    81, 82, 86-87, 96.

CLIVE CHAMPION:
    pages 4, 6-7.

RON ELMY:
    page 12.

FRANK GRANT:
    page 79.

JOHN SHERLOCK:
    page 84.

BOB WIGINGTON:
    page 61.

# Special Thanks

Fred Bird, Vicki Burns, Bonnie Cowan
Deborah Fadden, Christine Levac, Jennifer McLagan
Wanda Nowakowska, Donna Paris, Daphna Rabinovitch
Beverley Renahan, Kirk Shearer, Gord Sibley
Olga Truchan

# Index

# The Best Things in the Kitchen are the COOK'S OWN!

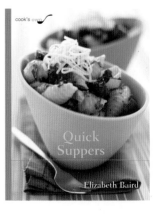